IT'S T
TRUTH

Making *The Only Ones*

Simon Wright

IT'S THE TRUTH

Making *The Only Ones*

Simon Wright

Shakspeare
EDITORIAL

First published by Shakspeare Editorial, UK, April 2023

ISBNs   pbk 978-1-7392549-0-2
        ebk 978-1-7392549-1-9

Copyright © 2023 Simon Wright

No part of this publication may be reproduced, stored in a retrieval system, or transmitted, in any form or by any means mechanical, electronic, photocopying, recording or otherwise without the prior written consent of the publisher; nor be otherwise circulated in any form of binding or cover other than that in which it is published and without a similar condition being imposed on the subsequent purchaser.

The right of Simon Wright to be identified as the author of the work has been asserted by him in accordance with the Copyright, Designs and Patents Act 1988.

Photography John Tygier (unless credited otherwise). In the case of some photographs it has not been possible to ascertain or trace the original copyright holders, if the photographers concerned wish to contact the publisher a credit will be included in future editions.

Editing Rebecca Thomas, www.thomasediting.co.uk
Design and typesetting www.ShakspeareEditorial.org

Dedication

For Wendy, Georgia and Bonnie

Dedicated to the memory of Mike Kellie, Koulla Kakoulli, Pete Makowski and Manuel Vardavas

My thanks to

Nina Antonia, Stuart Batsford, Richard Buskin, Steve Everitt, Peter Gravelle, Lawrence Impey, Alan Mair, Pedro Mercedes, Jon Newey, Peter Perrett, John Perry, Barry Plummer, Howard Thompson, John Tygier, Bob Whitfield and John Whitfield

All quotes are taken from interviews with the author unless otherwise credited

CONTENTS

Introduction 1
The Musicians Assemble 9
    Part One: Peter Perrett and England's Glory 9
    Part Two: John Perry 21
    Part Three: Mike Kellie 26
    Part Four: Alan Mair 34
First gigs 46
Recording Sessions 70
The Songs 90
    Side One 91
    Side Two 100
'Another Girl, Another Planet' 108
    Versions 119
And Then … 123
    The Sleeve 123
    Promoting the LP 127
    Faster Than Lightning 128
    Reviews at the time 129
    Reviews in retrospect 130
Epilogue 133
Bibliography 138

INTRODUCTION

I NEVER SAW The Only Ones live the first time around.

By the early 1970s, my home in the suburbs of South London was reverberating to the sound of nothin' happening at all. The waves of wonderful singles that had started in 1964 had tailed off and sod all had taken their place. The bands that played locally favoured denim boogie or plodding metal.

Then in November 1972, our local – Guildford Civic Centre – somehow managed to book Roxy Music, coming off their debut hit Virginia Plain. The band and their entourage were a revelation, both on stage and off ('Did you see the suits and the platform boots?'). Having inveigled our way into their dressing room, our teenage senses were completely blown by the glamorous people of all sexes, and free champagne served in proper glasses. No more Uriah Heep rock 'n' roll medleys for me.

Fast forward three years and I am experiencing a similar disorientation. This time the band on stage are a more straightforward proposition, though just as exciting both visually and musically. They are called the Sex Pistols and they are rapidly emptying our college hall. The difference is, when I look at Johnny Rotten I think 'I could do that.' This evening would later be documented by Clinton Heylin in his book

Anarchy In The Year Zero: The Sex Pistols, the Clash and the Class of '76.

Also intrigued by the activity around the Pistols camp were seamstress Xenoulla 'Zena' Perrett and her songwriter husband Peter, recently departed from his band England's Glory. Peter and Zena had met band manager Malcolm McLaren and his partner Vivienne Westwood in 1974, after being drawn to their boutique on the King's Road, variously known as Let It Rock, Too Fast To Live and Too Young to Die, and SEX, and later Worlds End.

Peter was a massive Bob Dylan fan but seeing the Pistols live at Chelsea School of Art in December 1975 made something more raucous a better bet. He said:

> 'I thought it was so funny that they did not give a fuck. It gave me the confidence that entertainment does not have to be completely musical.'

For my fashionable fifteen minutes in that summer of 1976, I was living in a bedsit in London's Queens Park, working at the McVitie's Bakery in Harlesden and attending every punk gig that I could. Gigs were the best way to hear punk. The short sharp shocks we had been craving were best delivered in person. There was the Screen On The Green All-Nighter and the Pistols' monthly residence at the 100 Club. At the two-day Punk Rock Festival at the same venue, I ended up next to Steve Jones – an occasion immortalised in Barry Plummer's pictures that would subsequently feature in many books and magazine articles. By then, the Damned, The Clash and The Buzzcocks were all gigging, as were the newly shorn Stranglers and Vibrators.

The Sex Pistols at The 100 Club Punk Rock Festival, September 20th 1976, author bottom left (Barry Plummer)

At about this time, Peter Perrett met John Perry – a professional musician on the West Country club scene since the age of fifteen, and a proficient guitarist of taste and restraint. Rehearsals at Manno's in Chelsea through the summer of 1976 prompted the recruitment of an experienced rhythm section of Alan Mair (Beatstalkers) and Mike Kellie (V.I.P.s, Spooky Tooth). This heady mixture of youthful naivety and experienced musicianship was named by Peter, with characteristic self-belief, The Only Ones. Released on the band's own Vengeance Records, 'Lovers of Today' was single of the week throughout the music press. Vengeance demonstrated Peter's attitude towards a record business that had reacted unfavourably to England's Glory.

Peter Perrett said:

'We were lucky that so-called punk happened, 'cos the rulebook had been ripped up. The one thing I had in common with punks was that I was quite angry. A lot of our early gigs ended in me smashing things.'

As soon as I heard 'Lovers of Today', I knew I had found my band. The quirkiness of the Velvets, the drive of Exile-era Stones, the economy of The Who; all my favourite bands were there but with an added urgency and a thoroughly unsettling lyric. The B-side, 'Peter and the Pets', strayed further into Lou Reed territory, albeit with its tongue firmly in its cheek.

Zena negotiated a deal with CBS. Good on paper, it was undermined by the A & R team that signed the band leaving immediately afterwards. To this day, John Perry believes that commercial success could have been achieved had the band gone with Island Records, where founder Chris Blackwell wanted to make them one of his personal signings, along with Steve Winwood and Bob Marley. Recording for The Only Ones debut LP was conducted across multiple studios from late 1977 into early 1978, with the LP released in April 1978. The opening track on *The Only Ones* served notice: here was a band that operated outside the dictates of fashion. Something urgent and edgy might have been expected. Instead, 'The Whole of the Law' is built on a gentle acoustic rhythm, languid sax and Perret's lyrical adaptation of Aleister Crowley. A pregnant pause gives added emphasis to the swelling introduction to the following track – 'Another Girl, Another Planet'. Had this been the enormous hit that was widely predicted, the career of The Only Ones would have been very different. *Allmusic* describes it as 'arguably, the greatest rock single ever recorded'.

'Breaking Down' has a jazzy swing and warm electric piano. 'City of Fun' is a more abrasive reading of a track first recorded by England's Glory and the side closes with 'The Beast', a cautionary tale of addiction and despair animated by multiple John Perry overdubs and the late entry of a brass section. The second side is a similar mix of upbeat tough talkers ('Creature of Doom', 'Language Problem') and more sensitive souls ('It's the Truth', 'No Peace for the Wicked') before the literary 'The Immortal Story' ends the set with more Perry guitar carnage. Also recorded around this time were: 'Oh No', 'In Betweens', 'Out There in the Night', 'Flowers Die', 'Special View' and 'As My Wife Says'.

Reviews for the LP in the weekly music press were ecstatic, mostly written by journalists who were by now friendly with the band. 'Can you say very superb?' was one tag line. Despite this and a CBS-promoted tour, 'Planet' failed to chart, twice.

Trash, Camden, Autumn 1977. Simon Wright, Keith Steptoe, Brian Devoil, Mick Brophy

By 1977 I was a singer in Trash, a four-piece band signed to Polydor. We released two singles – including one produced by the great Shel Talmy – but were remarkably unsuccessful. As a result I was too poor to go to any gigs, or buy any records.

The Only Ones continued to record for CBS and released two further LPs – *Even Serpents Shine* (1979) and *Baby's Got a Gun* (1980). John Perry claims they reached their peak as a live band during their 1979 US tour: a recording of the Chicago date bears this out.

By the time I had regained some financial stability, the band had paused their activities. That was 1981. The release of *The Peel Sessions* LP (Strange Fruit, 1989) and the excellent live sets *The Only Ones Live* (Mau Mau, 1989) and *The Big Sleep* (Jungle, 1993) kept up my interest in the band. They resumed activities in 2007 when Vodaphone used 'Planet' in an advertising campaign. Alan Mair used this as leverage to have Sony remaster and rerelease the three studio LPs and support the band touring the UK and Europe. The band have now once again ceased playing live and Mike Kellie's death in 2017 makes live dates more difficult. However this second bout of activity has allowed for a critical reappraisal of a band that linked the old wave with the new.

I'd decided that as a singer I made a good journalist, and began writing for pioneering London music magazine *Bucketfull of Brains*. In early 2007 I was offered the chance to interview John Perry ahead of the band's return to live dates, scheduled for the *All Tomorrow's Parties* festival to be held over the Easter weekend in April at Butlin's holiday camp, Minehead, Somerset. John mentioned they would play some sort of low-key warm up date before this. At the very last minute I got confirmation that the gig would take place in Ladbroke Grove on Sunday 15th April, with the band playing a handful of numbers after a set by Love Minus Zero, a group formed by Peter's sons, Jamie and Peter Junior. This presented me with a dilemma: here was my first chance to see a live gig by a band I had been listening to for thirty years but I was already committed to presenting an award at a black-tie dinner on the other side of town. I decided to do both. Amazingly it worked, although it meant I turned up at the gig in a sweaty heap and rather formally dressed.

Here's what I wrote at the time:

'The Inn on the Green off Portobello Road resembles a trustafarian youth club, a suitably incongruous setting for the first live performance by The Only Ones since 1981. Taking to the stage characteristically late – due apparently to difficulties rousing Perrett – the quartet delivered sturdy versions of "From Here to Eternity", "Miles From Nowhere", "The Whole of the Law" and (of course) "Another Girl, Another Planet" to an enthusiastic crowd of well-wishers and regulars. A broken bass string gave Perrett the chance for a solo version of a new song that might have been called "Is This How Much You Care?", to the seeming bemusement of the rest of the band. Teasingly, Alan launched into the opening riff of "The Beast", but closing time intervened. The rhythm section rocked and rolled, Perrett's guitar and vocals were highly effective and Perry played liquid lead guitar while apparently thinking about the cricket scores. By the time they get to the Shepherds Bush Empire in June spontaneous combustion must be a real possibility.'

The sold-out gig at the Empire that followed was indeed a very emotional affair. I had persuaded the band to let me DJ for them that night: a minute before they took the stage they asked me to introduce them. My rather bland *'Ladies and gentlemen ... The Only Ones!'* can be seen on the DVD the band released of the gig. John and I later agreed that in view of their legendary tardiness *'The latest rock 'n' roll band in the world ...'* would have made for a better intro. Of the eighteen tracks they played that night, eight were from the era of the first LP.

The Only Ones was not a commercially successful LP, peaking at number fifty-six in the UK album charts. It was never even released in the US. Instead, CBS America released *Special View*, a mishmash of random tracks from their first two LPs, with the addition of 'Lovers of Today' and 'Peter and the Pets'.

The production on *The Only Ones* is dense and has little sense of unity. The cover is dreadful. It is not even my favourite Only Ones LP – *Even Serpents Shine* offers a better selection of songs. However, *The Only Ones* presents a wonderful sense of possibilities and excitement, of a band standing on the verge of something fantastic. It also represents a road not travelled: what if the excitement and economy of the 1977 London scene had been grafted onto stronger musical roots? And the presence of 'Another Girl, Another Planet' illustrates how not being a hit can extend the shelf life of a song.

There is a lot to talk about ...

THE MUSICIANS ASSEMBLE

Part One: Peter Perrett and England's Glory

THE FOUR INDIVIDUALS who would form The Only Ones came from very disparate parts of the UK: Peter Perrett from Forest Hill in South East London, John Perry from Bristol, Alan Mair from Glasgow and Mike Kellie from Birmingham.

By his own admission, Peter was a highly intelligent but intensely disruptive youth who had been kicked out of two secondary schools and found succour in music. Talking to Amy Haben of *Please Kill Me* (2020) Peter Perrett reminisced:

'I discovered Bob Dylan at thirteen. Before that, it was the Beatles and The Kinks and The Yardbirds. It was all about the sound and the fashion, but Bob Dylan was the first person to articulate things that I felt were unique. So at fourteen, I started writing down words and I had a tape recorder and I'd make electronic tapes. These tapes were just me bashing a desk and chanting and turning them backwards and they sounded really weird to me.'

Peter Perrett, Waldram Park Road, Forest Hill, 1974 (© Lawrence Impey)

Bob Dylan provided the turning point, as he explained to Peter Jesperson in 2017:

'I was at a friend's house and he had an older sister and I heard "To Ramona". And I thought, I've never heard a voice like that. But I didn't have the record to play over and over. Then I heard "The Times They Are A-Changin" on pirate radio and I thought, I like what he's saying, the rebelliousness of it. Because I was a rebel from about the age of nine, so I associated with the ideas that he was proposing. But the changing point was when I heard "Like A Rolling Stone". That, just the whole thing, the sound, the vocal delivery. The intensity in the vocal delivery was like … that was the turning point.

'The next epiphany was in 1967, the summer of love. Syd Barrett's Pink Floyd, The Creation, early Fairport Convention, and The Incredible String Band were all groups that seemed really exciting, seeing them live as a fifteen year old. In September '67 I got the Velvet Underground's first album. "Heroin" was the first track … I didn't even think about the subject matter, I didn't know what it was really. I thought it was something that was dark and forbidden … but it was just the sound, it just sounded really dark and dangerous. And with the added bonus that he had a similar vocal delivery to Bob Dylan. They're worlds apart, but compared to everyone else that was singing, they were in their own little universe.'

Talking to Amy Haben of *Please Kill Me* in 2020 Peter remembers:

'my father did the one positive thing he ever did in my life and he bought me a drum. I used to bash this drum as hard as I could because I wasn't really a drummer. So, I think he was like, "Please, shut the hell up." So, in April 1969 he bought me a cheap acoustic guitar. I learnt two chords and started writing. I was seventeen, which was quite late to start.'

Other local music enthusiasts were the brothers Bob and John Whitfield and Jon Newey. They in turn would lead to Peter meeting his wife Zena. Bob Whitfield remembers that liking Dylan was the key:

'In 1965 my Dad ran a folk/blues/poetry club every Friday night at The Crypt at St Peter's Church, Streatham. The first night at the youth club I met a girl called Lorraine who was at Sydenham High School and she told her friend Zena Kakoulli that I really liked Dylan. I'd come back from school and there would be a phone call about 5 o'clock and my Mum would say "it's Zena" and we'd talk on the phone about Dylan. After about three or four months she came round and she was like the first bohemian hippy girl I'd ever encountered.'

Jon Newey would play a crucial part in bringing Peter and Zena together:

'In the latter part of 1968 I started playing percussion and drums. I used to go over to John Whitfield's parents' house with my first drum kit. John was a pianist, Alistair Kinnear was a really good guitarist. We played in the basement – Dylan songs and old blues things. I remember coming out one day and there was a boy, a bit younger than us with longish hair, sitting on the wall outside. He said he'd really liked what he heard. John said he'd seen him around Forest Hill. He introduced himself as Peter Perrett and asked if he could come down and listen at our next rehearsal. It turned out he lived with his parents round the corner. Zena Kakoulli was still at school and really into Dylan and she asked John Whitfield and I to back her for a few numbers at an end-of-school concert. Gordon Giltrap also played guitar for her, being her best friend's boyfriend.'

According to Nina Antonia in *The One and Only* (1996), Zena was with John when she first set eyes on Peter Perrett, walking up a hill towards them, 'with long straight hair and these full lips; he looked just like Jim Morrison. He totally ignored me because I looked like a school girl'. But she turned out to be the first girl Peter had met who was into Dylan and, back at John's flat, they got talking. In Zena, Peter gained a girlfriend and, it turned out, a lifelong partner and ally in promoting his music.

Zena Kakoulli

Jon Newey continues:

'Peter was a likeable lad – quite naive at the time. He wanted to get away from his parents. He was bright but very lazy. I remember going over there and his mother would say to me "Can you get Peter to wash?" and "Can you get him to get up earlier?"

The next step was for Peter to go electric. His first time on stage was some time in 1970 at a South East London College dance playing a six-string electric guitar with only four strings on a ten-minute version of "What Goes On", after which I ran off the stage.'

In 2005 Jon Newey told Nina Antonia how he had encouraged Peter's musical development:

'By 1971, Peter had grown up a lot. He wasn't the shy awkward boy I had known before. He said he'd been writing songs and asked me if he could play some. They were really striking. Peter had a strong voice and the songs were simple but very effective and grabbed me straight away. In the spring of 1972, Peter played me a bunch more songs and I thought they showed real promise. I said I'd like to hear them in a slightly more electric setting and his eyes lit up. Peter had never been in a band. He was just a bedroom guitarist at this point. I set about constructing a band around Peter to perform the songs. One day Peter brought Harry Kakoulli over. Harry was playing bass on an acoustic six-string guitar which he'd taken the top two strings off. He was quite an unexpectedly lyrical bass player and he worked very well with the structure of Peter's songs, despite his being completely inexperienced.'

Jon suggested they call themselves 'Peter and the Pets' but it was Perrett who ultimately christened the band England's Glory because as Jon explains:

'we believed we were the only band in England doing what we were doing. At a time of rather dull post-hippy pub rock, we were forging ahead with a new sound and in our young, slightly arrogant way we felt that it was the best new sound to come out of England, so the name fitted.'

(It was also the name of a popular brand of matches.)

The band began rehearsing at Underhill Studios in Greenwich. They were in good company: other clients included David Bowie and the Spiders From Mars, Iggy and the Stooges and Lou Reed and the Tots. Peter and Zena hung out with Lou and the Tots during their London visit in July 1972. Jon Newey recruited guitarist David Clarke, who had previously played with him in a band called They Bite. Instead of hawking demo tapes of England's Glory band around the UK's major record companies, Peter decided they would produce their own LP, made possible by the funds generated by Peter's rapidly developing drug-dealing business. Accordingly, in January 1973, England's Glory recorded ten tracks at Venus, a four-track demo studio (twin two-track Revoxes) in Whitechapel Road, East London. It took two, five-hour sessions at a total cost of £50, with the first session for the backing tracks, and the second session for vocals and backing vocals. Initially, eight acetates were produced, followed by twenty-five vinyl copies that were pressed and sold to friends for £4 each. Writer Pete Makowski remembers visiting Peter's flat during Only Ones' days and finding his speakers perched on a pile of England's Glory records. Eventually, in 1987, the tracks were released on vinyl as *The Legendary Lost Recordings* (Five Hours Back), coming out on CD in 1993 (Anagram/Cherry Red).

Zena took on the task of visiting record companies with the England's Glory LP in the hope of signing a record contract. All the major labels turned her down, including CBS and RCA. Typical was Miles Copeland at BTO:

> 'Sounds a bit like another Lou Reed, and there's not even enough room for one Lou Reed.'

There was a well-received gig at Anerley Town Hall in Bromley, South London, on March 23rd, which Peter later described as:

> 'the only time I'd ever been onstage, but that wasn't in front of the public. About 150 friends turned up and a couple of people who wandered in off the street.'

England's Glory, Anerley Town Hall

Soon after this, David Clarke left the band, only for David Sandison and Jonh Ingham at EMI to show interest in them, following a recommendation from journalist Richard Williams. A replacement guitarist called Julie was hastily recruited via an ad in *Melody Maker* and England's Glory Mark 2 recorded four further demos at the label's Manchester Square studios on June 8th 1973. The tracks were 'Predictably Blonde', 'Bells That Chime', 'Weekend' and 'Shattered Illusion'. Sandison's enthusiasm for the band was not shared by his boss Joop Visser and EMI passed (the tracks were eventually released on *The First and Last*, Diesel Motor Records, 2005).

Peter and Zena, Bournemouth 1976 (© Lawrence Impey)

Jon Newey said:
> 'Peter was becoming unreliable and Harry and I were both struggling through divorces and eventually inertia set in, although Peter, Zena and I continued our friendship.'

There was a further session in early 1974 using a recording set up above the Underhill rehearsal studios. With Gordon Edwards on guitar, Harry Kakoulli on bass and an unknown drummer, the tracks included 'Curtains For You', 'Predictably Blonde', 'Bells That Chime', 'Weekend' and 'Shattered Illusion'. Perrett claims 'they were all a million times better than the demos we did for EMI'. He also credits Edwards for the epic riff in 'Curtains For You', which would eventually be recorded for the second Only Ones LP, *Even Serpents Shine*. An early 1975 demo session with fellow South East London musicians Squeeze was recorded using a four-track in the Tooting flat of Andy Dalby from Arthur Brown's Kingdom Come. Songs recorded included 'Liar' and 'Cruel Sister', which later became The Only Ones' B-side 'Your Chosen Life'.

The Only Ones would go on to record three songs from the England's Glory LP – 'City of Fun', 'Peter and the Pets' and 'The Guest'.

Talking to *Sounds* in 1977, Peter Perrett said:
> 'England's Glory as a band were much more in tune with what's happening today than The Only Ones.'

– possibly because England's Glory sound to be totally in thrall to the Velvets. The England's Glory version of 'City of Fun' runs on an 'I Can't Stand It' rhythm track. The middle eight features a prominent piano and the song is taken at a more leisurely pace but otherwise the melody, lyrics and arrangement are similar to the version that The Only Ones would record five years later.

Though slower and more piano-based, 'Peter and the Pets' is a recognisable prototype for The Only Ones version. 'The Guest' never featured on an Only Ones album but was played live regularly by the band early on, and received an official release on the *Live in Chicago* CD. Acoustic demos of 'Flowers Die' (written in 1970) and 'In Betweens' were recorded by Jon Newey in his flat in Streatham in 1972. Featuring just Peter on acoustic guitar and vocals, they were ultimately released on *The First and Last*. There were two further consequences from the England's Glory experience. First, Zena would develop the managerial role she had explored with England's Glory into a full-time job as manager of The Only Ones. And second, the record industry's rejection of England's Glory would harden Peter's attitude towards them, to the point where the first Only Ones single was released on Vengeance Records.

Following the demise of England's Glory, there appear to be no recordings or gigs until June 30th 1975, when Peter supported The Global Village Trucking Company at London's Marquee. For this date he was again backed by Squeeze. The set was a mixture of England's Glory and soon-to-be Only Ones songs including 'City of Fun', 'Bright Lights', 'Your Chosen Life, 'First Time I Saw You', 'Weekend', 'I Only Want to Be Your Friend', 'Don't Hold Your Breath', 'My Rejection' and 'Out There in the Night'.

A surviving cassette tape recording of the gig shows Peter's voice and rhythm guitar are both strong. Despite some nimble bass playing, the songs tend to plod along in mid-tempo. They are embellished with intrusive Hohner electric piano and some lengthy guitar solos that add little to the songs. Overall the performance lies halfway between what England's Glory had been and what The Only Ones would become. The Marquee performance showed that what Peter really needed was a sympathetic musician who could turbocharge his singer-songwriter tendencies while respecting his idiosyncratic vision. Enter John Perry.

Peter Perrett at The Speakeasy, London, February 1977 (© Lawrence Impey)

Part Two: John Perry

COMPARED TO PETER, John Perry had a much less urban upbringing.

I grew up in Knowle, south of Bristol, where town met country. My mother was a teacher and we had long summer holidays in Porlock on the Somerset / Devon border. My father was musical, a decent amateur countertenor singer. He was into opera, which I have never taken to. I think he could have been a professional musician if he hadn't been the youngest of eight; they could not afford for him to go to college and study music. I assume general musicality is inherited.

'I first picked up an actual guitar in March 1966, although I had made a cardboard one before then. I was fascinated with The Shadows, Hank Marvin and his red Strat with the tremolo arm. Any guitarist of my age who says he was not inspired by Hank Marvin is lying. I remember learning the guitar part from "Substitute", "Sha La La La Lee", "All Or Nothing" and "Groovy Kind of Love". I liked the singles charts – the Beatles, Stones, Who, Hollies. From about 1965 you could hear pirate radio, notably Radio Caroline and Radio London, who played a wider range of stuff like The Creation. I favoured Radio London, especially when John Peel on the Perfumed Garden started playing West Coast stuff. Later I started listening to blues albums on Sue Records.

'I went to Cotham Grammar School. I had won scholarships to "leading schools" – Queen Elizabeth's Hospital, Bristol Cathedral Choir School, et cetera – but point-blank refused to go as they all did Saturday mornings. QEH boys, in addition, had to wear monstrous 16th-century monks' cloaks. So that was doubly out of the question. I played tympani in the school orchestra, where I learnt about ensemble playing; it gave me an insight into how sections interact. Ensemble playing is what separates people you want to play with from people you want nothing to do with. It's about listening. Some people just want to do their thing as loudly as possible.

'In Bristol, the only place you could go for lessons was the Spanish Guitar Centre, which didn't seem remotely attractive. I did have piano lessons and I was teaching myself guitar by ear, but I didn't link the two – they seemed as different as cricket and football. My first public appearances were in 1967, starting off as a guitar duo in the school hall with "the worst boy in the school". After that, in July 1967, I formed a three-piece band playing Cream and Hendrix stuff, which was interesting because the only places to play were British Legions and they did not want to hear bad copies of Hendrix. We would have to change the band name after each show to get rebooked.

'I became a professional musician at sixteen. My father was OK with this, either that or he was tired of arguing "let the boy do what he wants". My mother thought it was a disaster – "shouldn't you go to college so you have something to fall back on?" I don't think she ever understood it. The Bristol evening paper had a "musicians wanted" section. There was an early wave of Bristol beat groups, older guys who had been around in skiffle groups in the late 1950s, early '60s. For some reason they all seemed to be named after cars – Johnny Carr and the Cadillacs, Danny Clark and the Jaguars, Mike Tobyn and the Magnets – dozens more. These are guys who'd seen Eddie Cochran and Gene Vincent at the Bristol Hippodrome the night before the crash that killed Cochran. They had managers and organisation at a level I didn't have, so I started working with them, playing mainly covers at air bases, town halls and rugby club dances within a 100-mile radius. These guys knew about studios, so in 1969 we went off to Rockfield Studios in Wales, which was just being built, and did a bit of recording up there – tapes lost as far as I know. Around this time I was listening mainly to blues albums especially Elmore James and the English guitarists.

'In 1971 I played Glastonbury Festival with a band called Flash Gordon and fell in with the underground bands, which is where my natural tastes lay. For three years I toured with Magic Muscle, the Pink Fairies and Lemmy-era Hawkwind. We had a regular support slot at Bath Pavilion, where the promoter was Freddy Bannister, so we were playing with bands like Peter Green's Fleetwood Mac and Taste. We'd get about £20 a night for that.

'Flash Gordon lasted until 1972. Some people I knew who had been in California hanging out with Moby Grape and the 'Dead came back and introduced me to their circuit. We did a band called Over The Hill who overlapped in personnel with the Fabulous Ratbites From Hell. Both bands ran in parallel during 1973 to '74, the 'Ratbites being more of an R 'n' B band. Island were briefly interested in the 'Ratbites and Andrew Lauder at United Artists gave us some money to record at Rockfield.

The 'Ratbites at Trentishoe Festival 1973. Huw Gower, Big Pete, John Perry, Nick Howell (John Perry Archive)

'It was really cheap to live then. You could find a farmhouse that no one else wanted for £4 or £5 per week. I had a large house in Pensford with my girlfriend Maureen and her kid. At that point, unsigned bands were often supported by hash dealers who had some spare cash and felt philanthropic or by the odd aristocratic landed hippie. The 'Ratbites were guided by Bob Whitfield, who came from Forest Hill and had grown up knowing the Perretts. He organised some gigs and tours for the 'Ratbites in Holland in between conducting business there. He told us about this songwriter he knew in London who was looking for a backing band to play a show at the Marquee in the summer of 1975. Peter knew Squeeze and had tried them but Bob recommended he try the 'Ratbites. There was one rehearsal with Peter and the entire 'Ratbites line up. Zena decided they could work with the band but not that awful lead guitarist (ie. me). Bob urged them to reconsider on the basis they had it back to front.

'By November 1975 I had moved up to London and was living in Roehampton when I got a call from Zena asking if I wanted to do some demos in Tooting. The line up was Peter Perrett, Alan Platt from the 'Ratbites on drums, Gordon Edwards (Kinks, Pretty Things) on keyboards and Glenn Tilbrook from Squeeze on lead guitar – Glenn was living in Peter's house at this point. I played bass and overdubbed some guitar.'

The four Tooting demos were later released on the *Remains* LP (Closer,1987) where they were wrongly attributed to The Only Ones. The tracks were 'Watch You Drown', 'My Rejection', 'Don't Hold Your Breath' and 'I Only Wanna Be Your Friend'. There was also an early attempt at 'Out There in the Night'. These tracks are the earliest recordings made by Peter Perrett and John Perry to be released.

With the front line in place, the next requirement was a solid drummer. Cue Mike Kellie …

Part Three: Mike Kellie

MIKE KELLIE'S DRUMMING career began with Birmingham band The Locomotive, which featured Chris Wood on tenor sax and flute. In 2013 he summarised his career to date on www.mikekellie.com.

Mike Kellie at The Speakeasy, March 1977

Mike Kellie:

'Chris, Steve Winwood (Spencer Davies Group) and Jim Capaldi (Deep Feeling) were forming Traffic around the latter part of 1966. Chris Blackwell managed the Spencer Davis Group, his other group was the V.I.P.'s from Carlisle. They were a great rhythm and blues band and had come down to make it in London having conquered the north. Their drummer, Walter Johnson, missed his family and went back to Carlisle. I got a phone call from my friend Paul Medcalf, who said "Winwood wants to know if you're interested in joining this band … "So I was off, next day, straight from New Street Station, with my drums, to Paddington. Met by V.I.P.'s road manager, the legendary Albert Heaton, I was driven to 155 Oxford Street where I met Mike Harrison and Greg Ridley. I met the rest of the band later that evening.

'The next day I was in Paris playing at Olympia with the V.I.P.'s without any rehearsal! We were bottom of the bill – Chris Blackwell had done this deal for the band to open a star-studded variety fundraiser in aid of UNICEF. It was held at Paris Olympia and was televised worldwide, similar to the way All You Need Is Love was done. The V.I.P.'s had a single out in France on Fontana and we were over to promote it, a Joe Tex song called I Wanna Be Free. So I had no real rehearsal, just the journey over in the van. We did the TV show after I had phoned my mother from a post office in Paris earlier that day and said, "Mum, look in the Radio Times, I think we're on a TV thing tonight". The record became a big hit in France following that show.

'[The band] Art was formed because the lead and rhythm guitarists from the V.I.P.'s decided to leave, on their way back to Carlisle in Christmas 1966. That left Mike Harrison, Greg Ridley and me in need of a guitarist. So, in the same way that Winwood had recommended me, his then girlfriend, Penny, said "Why don't you try Luther?" Luther Grosvenor came down on the train with his guitar and an AC30, and we fitted like gloves. The name Art came about from there and we made what is now a very collectable album called *Supernatural Fairy Tales*. This was during the Summer of Love in 1967 and we were living in a flat in Sussex Gardens on a £12 a week retainer from Island Records. Guy Stevens, who was very much part of the Island family, produced the album.

'We continued playing in France and at the Star-Club in Hamburg as The V.I.P.'s and I remember we had a young Keith Emerson on keyboards for a few months. We only went out on tour as Art once, just after *Supernatural Fairy Tales* was released. The album itself was really just a collection of backing tracks rather than actual songs and although we'd been trying to pretend we were all songwriters, Chris Blackwell was starting to think "what do you do with a problem like Art?"

'While all this was going on, Steve, Jim, Chris and Dave Mason were getting ready to launch Traffic and they did a trio of warm up gigs in Sweden. The band supporting them in Stockholm was called The New York Times, with a guy singing and playing Hammond organ called Gary Wright, who Blackwell liked. So he brought them back to England, sacked the band and kept Gary. He brought us all into the office one day, introduced us and said "Right … last chance, you're going to make a band, what do you need?" So New Jersey boy Gary went to Harrods and bought a Baldwin electric harpsichord. He had this song called "Sunshine Help Me", which was very catchy and became our first single. We changed the name and Spooky Tooth was born. Jimmy Miller, a friend of Gary's, began producing both Traffic and Spooky Tooth albums. That continued until Jagger made Jimmy an offer he couldn't refuse!

'Spooky Tooth were being championed by people like John Peel and we toured the club circuit up and down the country. It was a vibrant time. The pirate radio ships really helped us. After that we went to Europe and then America beckoned. Traffic went over at the beginning of 1968 and we went over in the summer of 1968. It was a powerful band. The harpsichord on one side of the stage, Hammond organ on the other, Luther and Greg Ridley in the middle and me at the back.

'Johnny Hallyday used to come over to record his backing tracks with English musicians, sing the songs in French then release them in the French-speaking world. Mickey Jones was the guitarist with Hallyday's band in France and he knew Gary Wright. Gary got involved playing keyboards on some of these recordings and then asked me to come along and play, I guess because we were flavour of the month! This was all at Olympic Studios and that was how I met Johnny. So we did those recordings at Olympic with Peter Frampton on guitar, Pat Donaldson on bass, Gary on keyboards and me on drums. That's how I got to know Frampton and I played on his solo album after Humble Pie.

'Later on, studio engineer Chris Kimsey called me up and said "Do you want to do a tour with Johnny?" I must admit that I got a bit carried away on that tour, it was like touring with Elvis! Villages and towns throughout France would put up a big marquee for the gig and then great restaurateurs would take us back to eat afterwards. So having seen France on no money with the V.I.P.'s, I was suddenly seeing it with money floating around all over.'

Following the break up of Spooky Tooth, Kellie played sessions for Steve Gibbons, Johnny Hallyday, the *Tommy* soundtrack, the Jerry Lee Lewis London Sessions, Traffic, George Harrison, Peter Frampton, Joe Cocker, Andy Fraser and Paul Kossoff.

Manno's Rehearsal Studios forms the backdrop to the formation of The Only Ones. On the corner of King's Road and Lots Road in Chelsea, it was owned by Manolo Ventura from Lima, Peru, and was the rehearsal studio favoured by Peter Perrett. It was also where Mike Kellie was storing his drums.

He said:

'While at the studio one day Manno said to me "Kellie, there's someone I want you to meet … ". He was aware that I was looking for a songwriter, a front man; not looking for a band to join, but looking for a songwriter. He took me into one of the rooms. At this end was a blonde girl just sitting and at the other end were three guys playing music. John Perry was playing bass, Glenn Tilbrook was playing guitar and Peter Perrett was playing rhythm guitar and singing. We were introduced and got on really well and I enjoyed what I heard. That evening we went back to Kidbrooke, South East London, where Peter and Zena had a rented house. Peter played me his demos. That was it. I made a conscious decision – this is the guy I'm gonna play with! It was an interesting move but it was song orientated. Song and image. You can't carry the frontman and you can't carry the drummer. You can carry everybody else.'

John Perry is uncompromising in his assessment of Kellie:

'He was the best drummer I've ever played with. He came from the English, late '60s Ringo school of drumming – half-time licks, a very high class plain drummer. A big solid sound from his Ludwig kit. Kellie's drumming style was an odd mix. One side really solid, keeping it simple which I love – on the other side he would sometimes overplay, but even then he came up with some interesting stuff. The only time Kellie did dead straight, Simon Kirke-style drumming was on "Tall Stories", the single I did with him and Robert Palmer. Kellie himself said "Tall Stories" was atypical, although he did it beautifully.

'He was definitely a bit down on his luck when he met us, crashing at people's places along the Kings Road and storing his drums at Manno's. Manno tipped him off that we were a band with both money and songs. If you are a working musician you always come across dilettantes with money who want to record their songs and usually they are awful but it's something you do because it's an income. So around Easter 1976 Kellie came and introduced himself. I knew of Spooky Tooth but it was a band I wasn't really interested in. He claimed that he might want to produce us. Peter was impressed he'd been in Spooky Tooth and took him at his word. It quickly became apparent that drumming would be a better bet.

'It had been a while since he'd done anything that was successful and recent sessions with Paul Kossoff and the like were a bit marginal. I could see he was a bit scattered and in the early rehearsals he couldn't remember which song was which. People who have done a lot of speed earlier in their lives get quite scrambled and flustered. Once he felt secure in his role it was great to be playing with a drummer of his experience. Very professional in the studio. Always solid on stage. With a drummer as good as Kellie you've got space to play or not play and it still sounds good. I was used to counting songs in with previous drummers but Kellie definitely saw that as part of his role, setting the tempo. As an experienced drummer he had his area and defended it stoutly. Kellie never wanted to play a drum solo. He had a good sense of the songs.'

Peter Perrett remembers Kellie's ability to rapidly respond to songs he had not heard before:

'In 1977 I got a call from John Cale who was trying to contact Kellie as he had a gig in Coventry that night but no drummer. Kellie had never heard any John Cale material but I drove Kellie up to the gig, got him there half an hour before it started, he walked onstage and it was like he'd been rehearsing the songs for years. After the gig we went back to Cale's hotel and he spent the rest of the night trying to persuade Kellie to join his band.'

Manno's Rehearsal Studio, May 1976. Peter Perrett, Glen Tilbrook, Mike Kellie, Harry Kakoulli, John Perry (© Lawrence Impey)

John Perry:

'When it came to drugs he [Kellie] was a bit of a scrounger. His phrase was "Oh could I?" You'd be sitting out chopping out a line for yourself and this spectre would appear at your shoulder … "Oh could I?" …. Like someone who says they have given up smoking but has only given up buying cigarettes. I think Kellie had been used to having no money for a long time. Not a big indulger but took anything that was going. Never affected his performance, never screwed up his playing. He is a difficult man to talk about. What he did well is very apparent and it's there to hear. Always nicely turned out, conservative with a small "c". Terrifically Midlands. He had a tight circle of midlands pals who he stayed friends with throughout his life, like Stevie Winwood and Gordon Jackson.

John Perry recalls a photograph by Laurence Impey, taken at Manno's during May 1976:

'Everybody looks bored except Kellie, who's staring at Peter like a faithful spaniel. Glenn Tilbrook is sitting down with a white Strat. Peter kneeling on the floor, facing his amp, tuning-up. Harry Kakoulli playing bass.'

Tilbrook remained in the line up until one day John's exasperation at the excessive number of guitar notes being played proved too much and he pulled out Tilbrook's lead. *Exeunt* **Glenn. John Perry was now sole lead guitarist but with Harry off to Squeeze they needed a new bass player**

Enter Alan Mair …

Part Four: Alan Mair

ALAN MAIR GREW up in a musical household in South Glasgow.

'When I was seven we moved to my grandparents' house, one of my uncles had been to the US and he was into early R 'n' B. Playing the odd track by Don Covay, Big Bill Broonzy, Muddy Waters – all rhythmically very powerful. My dad was a fine piano and guitar player and he played Hoagy Carmichael songs, very cool and he sang like Mose Allison. When I was ten or eleven, one of my mates Willie Gaffney would buy a single every week on a Saturday. Every Saturday for a couple of years we would go to Willie's – me and Eddie Campbell – we would choose between us but he would buy it. The big game changer was "Heartbreak Hotel".

'Eddie got a guitar when I was twelve, so my Mum went to Glasgow Auctions and bought me an acoustic guitar for £12.50. I was ecstatic. By now The Shadows had arrived and Eddie was playing their songs. I learnt "Apache". I remember going out for "Bob-a-Job" night with my guitar and being invited into people's houses to play "Apache" for a shilling. Eddie and I talked about starting a band. He was going to play lead and I was going to play rhythm but one of Eddie's mates had already offered to play rhythm (he wasn't very good) so I said "that's cool, I love bass, so I'll play bass". My mum bought a bass on HP from McCormicks Music – a six-string Burns bass for £178. I thought it was perfect as I still had the desire to play melody.

'At fourteen, my best mate at school was Davie Lennox, he was always walking around singing so I asked him to try out for a singer. Davie messed up the audition due to his shyness but his second attempt at "From a Jack to a King" worked. By the time I was fifteen, I used to go ice skating all the time and they made me a steward. One of the other stewards was Hugh "Tudge" Wiliamson, a couple of years older than me, and a drummer. He auditioned using biscuit tins.

'Willie was always hanging around but didn't play an instrument so he became our road manager and his dad Joe was our manager and drove us around in his company van. Our first proper gig was supporting Frankie Vaughan when he came to open a new Jewish centre in Battlefield, Glasgow. We landed a six-week residency on Saturday nights at The Couper Institute in Battlefield, the Quintones played in the main room and we were in the small room where we were ignored until we turned our suit jackets inside out so the colourful lining was on the outside. The Quintones were the biggest band in Glasgow at the time – they wore gold lamé suits. Over the six weeks we got a wee following, girls starting to stop and watch us. The singer in the Quintones was Alex Ligertwood who became the singer in Santana.

'Next we started putting on our own gigs at Battlefield Scout Hall on a Sunday night. We were a bit mod-ish and there was no one else in Glasgow like us. By the end of 1964 we were filling the scout hut, so our next venue was the Baillieston Café on a Sunday night and three to four months later we were packing it out. Early in 1965 we restyled the band. We got a load of US 'n' B singles from Gloria's Record Bar – Solomon Burke, The Tams, Four Tops – and redid our whole set – nothing commercial, nothing British. We got girls screaming! All the songs in our set became hits two to three years later.

'We were asked to do a musical of *Jack and The Giant Beanstalk*. Davie was going to be Jack and we were going to be the Beanstalkers. That never came off, probably because we weren't very good. Eddie and I were sitting on a bus one day and talking about group names and we went from Beanstalkers to The Beatstalkers – "stalking the beat". From the Baillieston Café gigs just rolled in – selling out every club in Glasgow like the Elizabethan, the Barrowlands, then playing all over Scotland and if we played a second time it was sold out.

'When I was sixteen, I left school after my O-levels and Davie and I got engineering apprenticeships. Six months later, the band was playing every night. I was the only person with a driving licence, driving all night back from Aberdeen in the band's Zephyr 4 and going straight into the factory. Eventually I said to my Mum that I needed to turn pro, as I was earning ten times from the band what I was earning from my apprenticeship. In the summer of 1965 we handed in our notice and the managers said "you're throwing your life away". We made sure to drive past the factory at lunchtime in our flash Zephyr 4 when we knew the managers would be sitting outside watching the rest of the factory playing football.

'Joe Gaffney's nephew was a professional masseur in London. Producer Denny Cordell and John Fenton were among his clients – they came to see us at the Barrowlands and were blown away. Denny Cordell said: "I haven't seen this sort of audience reaction since Harlem". Denny got us signed to Decca in August 1965. When we left Glasgow to get the train to London to record our first single, 2,000 fans turned up to see us off, causing riots with hundreds of fans jumping on the track and trying to get on the train. Our first single, "Ev'rybodys Talking 'Bout My Baby", sold 200,000 copies which should have been enough to get in the charts but there were only two chart return shops in Scotland – one in Edinburgh, one in Glasgow – so that was never going to happen. We did *Ready Steady Go*, and a sold-out six-week residency at the Marquee with more people locked-out outside than they'd ever seen before, including hundreds of our fans from Scotland.

The Beatstalkers in the Necropolis Cemetery, Glasgow. Tudge Williamson, Davie Lennox, Ronnie Smith, Alan Mair, Eddie Campbell

'We wanted to record US songs like "Hey Girl Don't Bother Me", "Hang On Sloopy" and "Gin House Blues". Ray Davies was asked to write a song for us but Decca turned that down; they just wanted to use in-house songwriters all the time. Tony Washington was a black American songwriter and friend of Denny Cordell, so he wrote our first single. Denny's production company paid for the studio time and licensed the results to Decca. Davie was very nervous, Denny took a long time to get him to relax, but we got there in the end. We were as massive as we could be in any country – we had really conquered Scotland. We recorded three singles for Decca and then signed to CBS in 1967 for four more.

'Tudge was a miserable git. We were so enthralled with all this success: it was all you could ever want, driving nice cars, money in your pocket, go into a music shop, take out a wad of notes to buy something. We'd all bought flats when we were seventeen. Tudge was quite an old soul – he looks twenty years older in photos but he was only two years older than the rest of us. One day we were in rehearsals and he was sitting at his drums reading the paper and that was enough for Davie – there was a physical altercation and Tudge was out. We knew that Jeff Allen had played around Glasgow in some good bands so he joined.

'By now we were playing a lot in London and around England on US bases, then Germany and France. After the adulation in Scotland, it was a bit of a let down. I was twenty-one and we were about to go on tour. Jeff was driving the van, he stopped to go into a post office on the Holloway Road, came out and the van had gone with £3,000 of our gear including my Burns and my new Rickenbacker. We had discussions for two days before I said "guys, I am going to call it a day". We were now living in London and I didn't fancy borrowing three grand to start again. I went straight into making clothes. On the last trip we made to Germany I was already married and I wasn't a party person; I used to watch the landlady of our small hotel sewing and making things. Ken Pitt – David Bowie's then manager – offered me a room at his house in 39 Manchester Street. All I had to do was answer the phone as Ken Pitt Ltd. I knew enough musicians to think I could make a go of clothes.

'Ken was very masculine looking – like Clark Kent, tall, very square jaw – I had no idea that he fancied me. I was a pretty boy – a club owner in Germany had already offered me a Mercedes to go and live with him. I was at Manchester Street for about a year and it took a few months before Ken's feelings for me became obvious. He tried to get amorous with me one night and I said: "For fuck's sake Ken. What you doing? Back off".

'It really worked for me being in the West End – I was making clothes for so many bands – special flares with seams down the middle so the trousers dropped over your boots. Then leather trousers, leather jackets. Musician's wives would come in and say "can you make me a coat", so I went to John Lewis for a pattern similar to the style they described. Long fringe leather jackets – I made a load of stuff for The Marmalade's appearances on *Top of the Pops*. In 1969 I made clothes for Bowie who was also living in Manchester Square. I'd drive Bowie to his sparsely-attended gigs – Beckenham Arts Lab at the Two Tuns with an audience of less than ten people. Ken was starting to lose interest in Bowie, who was becoming a bit of a hippy, taking acid. David wrote a song about my little boy Frank, called Little Bombardier, which would open side two of his debut LP in 1967.

'In 1969, a friend of mine said I should take a stall in Kensington Market, which I'd never heard of. She managed a poster stall there. So I went down and was amazed – clothes were on the ground floor and downstairs, antiques on the first floor. But the only shop unit I could get was on the first floor, £15 per week. It was called Death Row because clothes never sold there. I had rented a little flat in Kentish Town and I was making clothes there as well as Manchester Street. My landlady in Kentish Town had a sewing machine, so in a week we made fifteen pairs of leather trousers and hung them up to make the shop look less empty. In the first week we sold nine pairs – £5 to make, sold for £15 – £90 then was a good wage! And it grew from there. In April 1969 I found a factory and my landlady became the manager.

'Then a guy came in and said "can you make me a pair of boots in the same leather?" – I had loads of offcuts – and I drove around London until I found Demetri who was in Pratt Street. He made a pair of boots for me for £8, I put them up in the shop and everybody went nuts for them so the boot thing exploded and I went back to Demetri and said "I need forty pairs". Moved the factory over to just making boots. There were queues of people on a Saturday at Kensington Market waiting for my boots to arrive, took over half a shop on the Kings Road and another shop in South Kensington, selling wholesale to Carnaby Street, selling to Italy and Germany. Thousands of pairs of Alan Mair branded boots.

'Kensington Market had a football team. We played in Regents Park and no one there knew how well I was doing until I turned up for a match in a 1969 Mach 1 Mustang – black bonnet, sky blue metallic. Other shop unit owners would say, "What the fuck are you selling?" I was twenty-two. By now Freddie Mercury was working for me while Queen were starting up. Long hair, Afghan coat, Mustang – I was a man around town, rockstar style. Freddie told me "I was at a party on Saturday and everyone had your boots on – boys and girls. You are not cool unless you have a pair of AMBs!"

'Fashion had been as much fun as music and I had enjoyed four years of profitable business and the excitement of working for myself. But it was getting repetitive, so I went down to Denmark Street and bought myself a new bass. I had only written one song for the Beatstalkers – Sugar Chocolate Machine, the B-side for the David Bowie-penned Silver Tree Top School For Boys. I was doing no music at all. I had a Gibson JB25 twelve-string I played for pleasure at home for friends but at twenty-one I thought making rock 'n' roll was best left to teenagers.

'My friend Norman Watt-Roy said to me: "Alan you should be back playing. I'll come over with Ollie (drummer from Average White Band) and we'll do some demos." That was so much fun. I had no confidence in my song writing but Norm said "you're writing great songs, you should get back playing". Although I was married with a young son, I had done well enough from my boot business for them to be looked after and supported for the foreseeable future. I was twenty-six and I thought if I don't go back to music I am going to regret this for ever.

'I sold half my business. I started playing in The Cock Tavern in Edmonton on bass with a band called Can Can, without telling anyone, just to get fluent. Next was a gig with the Al Matthews Band, still playing for fun. After a year I thought "my playing is getting good", I was ready to take the next step. In 1976 I started replying to the "musicians wanted" pages of *Melody Maker*. The first band I auditioned for weren't very good but the second band were, Chapman-Whitney Streetwalkers, and I had loved Family since seeing them at a psychedelic all-nighter supported by The Action.

'The audition was at Manno's. I was in the reception area where I could hear Peter's voice, sounding very Lou Reed, and he came out with two stunning girls, one of whom was his then girlfriend. Then the band came out and I knew Mick the bass player from the 'Cock but he said "it's not my kind of thing, I'm just helping out doing some demos". The two mini-skirted girls went back into the room and I thought, "well, I know the bass player, so I can wander in". So I watched the band and I recognised Kellie the drummer from the V.I.P.s. The Beatstalkers had played a lot in the border towns such as

Dumfries: The V.I.P.S were from Carlisle so they used to do that circuit as well, they'd supported us. So I knew Kellie's face. I was friends with Jon Anderson from Yes around then and they had played the Royal Albert Hall, supported by Spooky Tooth, so I had gone backstage and saw Kellie. I thought he was a really good drummer.

'So when I wandered into their rehearsal room, Kellie was the face I knew and Kellie clocked me and we had a spiritual connection – we liked the look of each other. All done on Kellie's intuition. He asked "Who was that guy?" I had already left but he got my number from the office. Even when he rang I said "I'm going to pass, I'm not too bothered, I feel like playing some guitar". Kellie said come and have a play, so I did – probably to see if that girl was still around. We played for two to three hours and we only really clicked musically once. Kellie rang me again and I said "I'm still not sure". Kellie said "come down to the house in Kidbrooke, we've got some demos for you to hear". I was on my way to somewhere else so I dropped into the house.

'After about two hours Peter had not emerged from the bath, so I was about to go. Then Peter's girlfriend Lynne came back and, just as I was about to leave, Peter turned up being very sweet, saying "I am so sorry I kept you waiting. I was waiting for someone to wash my hair, you know what it's like". And I thought "this is really different". Then they put on Out There In The Night and everything changed. Being a lover of lyrics I thought "wow, this fantastic, I love this". Then, Watch You Drown – the voice really surprised me. I made up my mind there and then. I officially joined the band over dinner in Fulham on August 13th, 1976.'

First band photo session. John, Peter, Alan and Kellie

FIRST GIGS

WITH THE BAND assembled it was time to work up a set for live gigs. John Perry admits it took longer than expected:

'We spent the whole of 1976 rehearsing at Manno's, principally because Peter had never gigged and so was more nervous than he would admit. We had a small Acoustic PA which Peter lent to Manno in exchange for us getting free use of the studio. I have never known any band that rehearsed for that long before starting to play live. There were benefits for having rehearsed that much – we knew the songs backwards, which was good. From the first gig all the improvement we made after that – and it was rapid – came from playing in front of people. We couldn't have gained much more from playing in a rehearsal room.

'We didn't find Alan until August, so only five months was rehearsing with him but as far as I was concerned it was thirteen months from first rehearsal to first gig and that was too long. Some songs lost their edge during the extended rehearsal period but we rested them and they came around again. An example was The Guest. Peter wrote rather a lot of songs that were basically the Sweet Jane chords, this is one of them. B-list.'

According to Martin Lawson (2001) a return to Tooting Studios in August 1976 produced versions of 'Breaking Down', 'River of No Return', 'In Betweens', 'Peter and the Pets', and 'Hope Valley Blues'. (The latter is a list of places in Australia, written by Peter for a girl who emigrated to get away from him). 'Breaking Down' is the version that appears on *The Only Ones*. All the other tracks except 'Peter and the Pets' would later appear on the *Remains* compilation LP.

Around this time John got to grips with the acoustic version of 'Flowers Die':

> 'It was the first song Peter ever wrote but it needed an arrangement, so I added a more delicate intro with a heavier riff. Great song. Always went down well at gigs. It might have been a good inclusion on the first album. The best version was recorded for Nicky Horne at Capital Radio.'

According to Peter, this is the version that is included on *Remains*.

The Only Ones were formally launched to the world in December 1976 at a party held at Summa rehearsal studios in Lots Road (now the 606 Club), just round the corner from Manno's. In attendance were Vivienne Westwood, Billy Idol, Tony James, Siouxsie, Glenn Tilbrook and Chris Difford. A three-piece Generation X followed The Only Ones set.

Alan and Peter, launch party, Summa studios, December 1976

Peter and John, launch party, Summa studios, December 1976

The Only Ones made their live debut at The Greyhound in Fulham on January 14th 1977, a gig secured due to Alan's friendship with the landlord. Because Peter was nervous about his rhythm guitar playing, a pianist called Norman was hired for the evening but he added little and was not used again. Audience members included singer songwriter Sandy Denny and American producer Terry Melcher.

First gig. Peter, Alan and John at The Greyhound, Fulham, 14 January 1977

First gig. Peter, Alan, Kellie and John at The Greyhound, Fulham, 14 January 1977

The Speakeasy

The Speakeasy, March 1977

The band's second gig was at music-biz hangout The Speakeasy, where thanks to Mike Kellie's friendship with manager Jim Carter-Fea, they were given a residency that ran from March through to September 1977. This was another key development, as Peter Perry explains:

'Once we started playing at the Speak' we were effectively members and we hung out there a lot, using it like our own youth club. Plus all the A & R men hung out there so we never had to petition them, they came to us.'

The Speakeasy, March 1977

Writing to John Perry on MySpace, Steve Brickle was impressed by a Greyhound gig in early March. He wrote:

'The band were simply stunning and on a lot of levels more powerful than the later gigs. As you were on stage it would not have been really possible for you to have been aware of the waves of sound that the band generated towards the back of the venue – quite extraordinary.'

The Speakeasy, March 1977

The Speakeasy, March 1977

Other early London dates included The Roxy on February 25th and the Marquee on March 28th, the latter supporting The Heartbreakers, thanks to their burgeoning friendship with founder of the New York band, Johnny Thunders.

John Perry:

'During the spring run of Speakeasy gigs, Thunders came down and introduced himself, I remember him in the little dressing room behind the stage. Nobody in the band much liked the music of the [New York] Dolls but we all knew who The Heartbreakers were. Thunders latched on because we were another real band. The bands who were on the Anarchy in the UK tour he didn't really consider competent musicians, apart from the Sex Pistols. He knew of Spooky Tooth, so he approved of Kellie – he used to go to virtually every gig at the Fillmore East.'

Peter Perrett was also impressed. Talking to Thomas H. Green of *The Arts Desk* in 2015 he said:

'Johnny was a friend. We had similar interests, in as far as we liked taking the same drugs. He had good taste in clothes and music. He introduced himself to me saying, "My name is Johnny Thunders, I love your voice". He flattered me so much. It was the first time a man had seduced me into wanting to talk to him. Back then, if you weren't a girl there was no reason for me to want to talk to you. He'd read that Keith Richards had been listening to our music so he came to a gig out of interest and we became friends.

'He always represented to me the darker side of what I could be if I fucked up. I've got this terrible reputation but when I used to play with The Only Ones I never used to take drugs. When it came to doing music it was too important – why would I want to take drugs? Maybe afterwards to keep the high of being onstage. That's what eventually sucks you in, especially when you get success – 2,800 people at the Lyceum treating you like you're God. The adrenalin takes you to a high place. With Johnny, he was like Mr Hyde to my Dr Jekyll.

Peter and John at The Marquee, 28 March 1977

Alan and Peter at The Marquee, 28 March 1977

John Perry had little time for the other London bands then being referred to as punk:

'Peter had more time for Vivienne and Malcolm but I had no time for this "year zero" shit. I certainly wasn't going to stop liking Arthur Lee or Jimi Hendrix. I enjoyed the Pistols when I saw them.

'The Clash at the 100 Club Punk Festival – or any of those gigs where we hired them our PA – were a tinny, screeching racket with no bass. Strummer couldn't string two sentences together without contradicting himself. When the Pistols played at the festival I thought the whole thing went up from the Third Division to the Premier League. I remember talking to Dave Goodman who was running the desk that night. I was saying something about the mix and he started knocking the faders around all over the place and saying that it didn't matter with this stuff.'

In later years, Peter would record a version of Ray Davies' 'I'm Not Like Everybody Else', which could be his theme song. As he told Peter Jesperson in 2017:

'From the time I was nine I thought, "I'm different from everyone else" ... and I felt disconnected from the world. I always felt that there was something ... that I was special in some way, hence when I dreamt the name it was The Only Ones. I just felt that we had to be different from everything else. And, luckily, at the time we came together, it was easy to be different from everybody else because all the other new bands were people like me – just starting to learn how to play.

'There were lots of good people that came on the scene that turned into great bands, like The Clash. Lots of people became great bands but, at the beginning, there weren't many that had lead guitar breaks, especially a thirty-two-bar intro to a song, like "Planet". So it was very easy to stand out. Number one on the agenda was to be different from everybody else. That was THE most important thing. Which is why I wanted to be as different from my heroes as possible back then. So, it did feel like we were unique. Because Alan and Kellie were in the band, there was a connection to what had come before. But because of my sort of chaotic approach to stuff, it had a relevance to what was going on at the time as well. I think the combination made us stand out.'

A recording of a typical rehearsal at Manno's was made on a pair of Revox two-track machines on June 2nd 1977 and John Perry confirms it is a pretty faithful picture of how the band sounded at that time. The tracks are: 'I'm Yours', 'This Ain't All It's Made Out To Be', 'Prisoners', 'As My Wife Says', 'The Guest', 'Watch You Drown', 'Lovers of Today', 'In Betweens', 'Another Girl, Another Planet', 'The Whole of the Law', 'Oh No', 'Peter and the Pets' and 'City of Fun'. Even at this early stage here was a unit that functioned effectively live and utilised simple but effective arrangements to allow Peter Perrett's distinctive vocals to be heard. Out of the thirteen tracks here, three would be B-sides, three were destined for the first album, one song would appear on the second album and five tracks would not appear on any of the three studio albums: there was little relationship between when songs were written and when they would be released.

Writing on MySpace, John Perry was particularly fond of this rehearsal take of 'Prisoners' for its feel, mistakes and all:

'Feel trumps error, every time. "Prisoners" was probably written at a time when Peter was attracting a lot of heat. It was getting heavy and there were real concerns over his liberty so a plan was started (though typically never finished) to stockpile material in case Her Majesty decided to entertain Peter at her pleasure for eighteen months or so.

'Built around a four-bar loop, "Prisoners" differs from much of Peter's writing on two counts. First, he rarely squeezed this many chords into four bars. Second, there are moderately complex chords here he didn't often use, an A6 and an augmented D. But this isn't prog. The chords are these because that's where the tune takes them, rather like Lennon and his strange time signatures, they are never there to show off technique, they are there simply because that's how many beats are needed to fit the lyric in. This was the first song Peter wrote on piano, hence the different chord voicings. It's taken at *the* perfect tempo – Alan and Kellie have it nailed – you can hear that from the relaxed feel of the band and especially Peter's diction. No stress required to phrase the words. This version is where I hit on that ladder of rising notes towards the end. I say I "hit" but it's really the whole band responding as one to that glorious moment of tension/release at the song's pay-off line: ...*confined within a space so small / we helped each other OVER THE WALL* ...

'Kellie sets up the tension with a half-time drum fill (2:45) and the intensity builds for about sixteen seconds until it subsides into an adapted version of the guitar hook from another song about going away, Cliff Richards' "Summer Holiday". This was the version Keith Richards heard and liked.'

Introduced by Steve Brickle, Keith Richards was sufficiently impressed to visit recording sessions in Tooting and Basing Street but ultimately passed on the chance to work with the band. Richards was also responsible for *Sounds* journalist Pete Makowski's interest in the band:

'At *Sounds* I sat next to Barbara Charone, she was very close to Keith Richards as she was writing a book on him and she said there is this band The Only Ones who he is interested in producing, will you go down to the Speakeasy and see them play? I absolutely adored them straight away. They reminded me of a punky rock 'n' roll band who had not been stylised to present an image. The Only Ones seemed perfectly formed from the first time I saw them. They were a cut above the rest. Barbara got me the "Lovers of Today" single which I reviewed for *Sounds*. I was an instant fan.'

Also in June, The Only Ones played their first tour dates outside London. John Perry remembers:

'A strange set of dates that Zena set up in early June. It started in The Manor Hotel outside Bridgwater, then Saturday night at a working men's club in the Valleys, then a rugby club in Newbridge the next night. I grew up playing those places so I knew what we were supposed to do. At first the audience didn't like it then Peter got bolshy and started kicking over mike stands and they liked that.'

Peter Perrett:
'In 1977 the way I was approaching music was just to play as loud as possible, to try and damage people, not let them off easily. Being in tune wasn't a priority, I felt I should go onstage and express all my demons. I felt like it was me versus the world. I had a lot of pent-up anger through having been sent away to boarding school. It all came out!'

First-hand accounts

A first-hand account of seeing The Only Ones at this stage is provided by John Tygier:
'I was on my year out from college, working in the architects department in the London Borough of Lambeth. My girlfriend Sharon was running events at the University of London so I saw a lot of bands, two or three a night. I went down to the Fulham Greyhound one evening to photograph a band called Snatch – [New York punk girl duo Judy Nylon and Patti Palladin] – who were playing with The Only Ones. In those days people with big Nikon cameras were quite rare and Judy came over to me and said Patti's

boyfriend is a photographer and doesn't really like people photographing the band, but she introduced me to Zena. What I agreed with Zena was that I would go to Only Ones gigs, take some photographs, print out the good ones and put my name on the back. Zena gave them to music papers and eventually a cheque for £7 would come through from IPC, which just about paid for the film. I only photographed them once or twice at the Speakeasy because it's not that kind of place.'

John's photo of the band playing at the Speakeasy accompanied their first reviews in the music press. (Patti Paladin's boyfriend was Peter Gravelle, later the photographer for *The Only Ones*.)

John Tygier:

'They weren't like other bands, they were older than most. They weren't pretending to be anything. They also had a slightly New Yorky edge. Peter's voice doesn't have English mannerisms, more a drawl. John had his Modern Lovers T-shirt which was making a statement. Mike Kellie was a phenomenal drummer, a musical drummer – not just thrashing out the beat but playing the song. There was a seriousness about them – before they went on stage, while they were on stage and after they'd been on stage. They didn't have youthful ambition. Although I was backstage with them … the photographs I could have taken!'

In September, The Only Ones had their first experience of larger stages, supporting The Stranglers on tour for five dates. John Tygier went to photograph the Oxford Polytechnic date on September 26th:

> 'I came back in John's Rover with Johnny Thunders. Thunders slipped me a tablet and I woke up on my drawing board the following lunchtime.'

Supporting The Stranglers September 1977.
top: Alan, Peter, John and Kellie; bottom: Alan and Peter

Hanging Out With Rebecca and Barbarella

Stuart Batsford was an early fan of The Only Ones. Now a successful record executive specialising in re-releases, he remembers the first time he saw the band.

Stuart Batsford:

'In 1977 I was eighteen. All my money went on records and gigs. Every Saturday I'd go into Birmingham and go round all the record stores. I was going to a hundred gigs a year and there was no one to touch The Only Ones. They were the best by a long way. With The Only Ones I never knew what they were going to play or what order they would play it in. They never seemed to have a setlist. They pulled a mixed audience, with good looking women because of Peter – I know my girlfriend fancied him. Loved their dress sense – Peter wearing baggy pink pantaloons tied at the bottom, a girl's blouse and eyeliner. Kellie was an old rocker. John clearly didn't give a fuck about what anyone thought of what he wore – usually cricket whites.

'I first saw them on July 27th supported by Snatch at a small club in Birmingham called Rebecca's. To my mind they were just another punk band who'd put out a single I'd bought without hearing ('Lovers of Today'), which sounded a bit more rocky than most of the punk singles I'd bought. The second time … was April 13th 1978 supporting Television at Birmingham Odeon. They blew Television off the stage. I'd seen Television the year before playing [their album] *Marquee Moon* live and it was, like, wow! But a year later they looked jaded and tired, couldn't follow The Only Ones, didn't have their power or attack.

'[Next was] Barbarella's, another Birmingham venue, on the 24th May, 1978. By now I really liked the band and I wanted to see them headline a show. There were about a hundred people there. Came on at 11pm, opened with "Watch You Drown" – the slowest thing you can imagine – then – bam! – into "City of Fun". They were so great in 1978. For me, the debut LP is perfection, a ten out of ten record. But they never really promoted it as a record. At all The Only Ones gigs I went to – and I went to a lot that year – they played tracks not on the LP like "Someone Who Cares", "Oh No" and "As My Wife Says".'

The Peel Sessions

The band recorded their first session for John Peel on September 13th, 1977. The tracks recorded were 'Oh No', 'Lovers of Today', 'Telescopic Love' (later renamed 'Special View') and 'In Betweens'.

John Perry is a fan:

'The Peel Sessions swing more. They were great because they illustrated just how good we were live and that we spent too much time fiddling around with tracks in the studio when we were making the actual records. There is a lot to be said for recording a live vocal performance from start to finish.'

In his book on Radio One radio sessions (1993) Ken Garner quotes Perry as saying:

'when somebody wanted to know what we sounded like, I'd always play them the Peel Sessions in preference to the studio albums. They're rougher but there's more feel, because the songs were more or less recorded live. You could do more or less whatever you wanted; nobody was at all put out when I wanted to record the sound of my Strat being thrown around the room for "Oh No". They just went out and set up the appropriate mikes. The great thing about recording under these conditions and at that speed is that it shows up whether the songs stand up for themselves.'

'Oh No' is a welcome reminder that the band had a frivolous side and they play this version with yobbo joy. 'Lovers of Today' contains twin guitars playing in unison but it's a long way from Wishbone Ash. Peter sings the line *'you could say things get pretty tranquil with me'* with great emphasis – the lyric about an asexual relationship sounds increasingly contemporary.

'Telescopic Love' sounds like Kevin Ayers singing 'Caribbean Moon', Peter having something of Ayers' approach and presence as well as his love for a double entendre (*'this thing is going to get bigger'*). 'In Betweens' features in the arrangement that would be used on the second LP, right down to John Perry's electronic emulation of a seagull.

A second session for John Peel was recorded on April 5th and broadcast on April 14th, 1978. The songs played were 'Another Girl, Another Planet', 'The Beast', 'No Peace For The Wicked' and 'Language Problem'. 'Planet' is very close to the recorded version, right down to Peter's 'woo-hoo' over the start of the guitar solo. 'The Beast' lacks its usual coda but features a more inventive bass line from Alan. 'No Peace For The Wicked' again follows the recorded version closely. 'Language Problem' is frantic fun and features one of Peter's best-ever one liners '*I love my mother but I wouldn't want to have sex with her*'.

Front Row Festival

From 22nd November to December 15th, 1977, the Hope & Anchor in Islington hosted *The Front Row Festival*, organised by pub manager John Eichler. He persuaded twenty-two well-known bands to play only for expenses as a way to keep the pub going. The Only Ones played on December 6th and the whole gig was recorded on a twenty-four-track mobile studio.

John Perry remembers the gig as shocking:

> 'It was so full and so hot that everything was way out of tune. The track that went on the album ("Creature of Doom") had to be completely reconstructed, the only thing we kept was the drums.'

This is the first good quality recording of The Only Ones live and, listening to it today, the set sounds better than John remembers. There are problems – the band repeat 'Another Girl, Another Planet' for unspecified reasons and the sound on the opener 'The Whole of the Law' is decidedly murky, it improves thereafter. The other songs played were 'In Betweens', 'Lovers of Today', 'As My Wife Says', 'It's The Truth', 'Oh No', 'No Peace For The Wicked', 'Language Problem', 'Peter and the Pets' and 'City of Fun', plus encores of 'Special View' and 'The Gallery'. 'It's The Truth' was rarely played live and it features a guitar part very different to the recorded version. Even a relatively minor song like 'The Gallery' benefits from an ending where the band move up a gear. The guitar solo in 'No Peace For The Wicked' is as brief as it is effective. 'As My Wife Says' comes in well below two minutes but never degenerates into thrash. Overall, a fine depiction of the band's live prowess at the end of 1977. A double live LP taken from the festival recordings was released by Warner Brothers in March 1978: the credits referred to 'Creatures of Doom' and Peter went apeshit (allegedly). John Tygier took the photos of The Only Ones featured on the sleeve.

Zena and Peter backstage at the Hope & Anchor, 6 December 1977.

Backstage at the Hope & Anchor, 6 December 1977.
top: Ludo (roadie), John and Kellie
bottom: Keeth Paul (soundman), John and Alan

*Zena and Keeth Paul backstage at the Hope
& Anchor, 6 December 1977*

The final gigs of the year were supporting Eddie and the Hot Rods. John Perry:

'Great gigs – really good PA, good monitors and we could work a big stage by then. It felt like a step up. Alan and I were both getting "good band but why don't you get rid of that terrible singer?" from our musician friends but the Roundhouse shows put an end to that.'

RECORDING SESSIONS

THE ONLY ONES were financially independent throughout their career due to funds generated by Peter and Zena Perrett's drug dealing. This meant they could record in much better studios than most unsigned bands.

John Perry:

'Most bands would book a month or six weeks and record pretty steadily, what we were doing was going into the studio whenever we had a song. A much better way to do it if you can afford it. Peter could have taken the same set of songs and recorded them with any bog-standard punk band: the compositions would have been as good but they would have been a much less enjoyable listen. Peter absorbed the idea that if you get good enough musicians there is no need to tell them what to play and it worked for two and a half albums.

'Peter would either demonstrate new songs on an electric guitar not plugged in or, most likely because we were rehearsing so much, he would just start playing them at rehearsals and we would have fallen in and found parts. We never spoke about arrangements. I might have an idea for an intro, a coda or a break but otherwise it was largely unspoken – we just played them. Generally the backing tracks went down well because we were well rehearsed and a good live band. Or we'd do twenty takes and it would turn out that the first one was the best. We would generally get the basic song down playing live with Peter doing a guide vocal at the same time, sometimes we would only keep the drums, then add bass, then add rhythm guitars and build up from there.

'We had the self-belief that anything we played was good and if it wasn't we'd hear it, which is why certain songs got dropped. No one ever criticised anyone else. My own playing came on fast because Alan and Kellie were such a good rhythm section – I'd been stuck in Bristol for the last couple of years and I could not get any further because you can't get further than the drummer. Peter had a good sense of time so there were no problems there.'

Alan Mair said whereas he and Kellie both came from bands that had done a lot of touring:

'Peter had an innocence with his lyrics and his approach, and John had his wide musical tastes. If Peter had come from the same era as me and Kellie we would not have had the diversity. Like The Who – four very diverse characters but put them together and it makes sense. The Who were my first big influence when the Beatstalkers were doing TV shows with them, playing "I Can't Explain" and "My Generation". I recognised the same strength in Peter Perrett's rhythm guitar playing.'

While drugs were always part of The Only Ones, Pete Makowski did not feel they were having a significant impact at this point:

'John was always a very functioning drug addict. Cricket probably took up as much of his time as heroin. It was like a previous era when people dressed very elegantly and went to parties but they just happened to have a laudanum habit.

'It is not unusual for bands to be formed on black market economics. Peter was very immersed in the dealer lifestyle. I've never really got on with dealers as they have a sort of rock star life without the music. They have to be underground. I used to live with a woman from Boston who was a dealer and I met more musicians living in a squat in Acton than I did at *Sounds*.

'The upside is that Peter was a visionary, he looked good and he picked the right musicians. There is a period on drugs where that all worked and that was Pete's Only Ones period. People who liked The Only Ones were quite devoted to them but the reason that didn't translate into sales was the lack of work ethic and single-mindedness. Selling more records wouldn't have helped.'

'Lovers of Today'/'Peter and the Pets'

The first Only Ones single was 'Lovers of Today', backed with 'Peter and the Pets', released on the bands own Vengeance label. The release date is given variously as June, July or August 1977. The initial pressing was 500 twelve-inch vinyl singles and without a distribution deal in place it is likely they trickled out to shops over this period. Both songs were credited to Peter Perrett.

The tracks were recorded over three or four sessions late at night, upstairs at Island Records' Basing Street studio in Notting Hill Gate. John Perry:

'We'd been recording in mid-price studios, so this was a step up. Basing Street was an old church with a huge studio, a big live area that could accommodate a sixty-piece orchestra or 100-piece choir. Most of our live takes were done up there. Downstairs there was a kitchen, a pool room and a small studio suitable for overdubbing single instruments. It should have been a mixing room but the sound was terrible – everything you mixed there came out bass-light. Either we mixed upstairs or we did it elsewhere.'

Peter had already recorded at Basing Street in 1975 – before The Only Ones sessions – so he was familiar with both the studio and engineer Robert Ash.'

Robert had a deal where he could bring bands in he liked during studio downtime, which was from midnight to whenever the cleaners came in. Songs recorded included an early version of 'Counterfeit Woman' and another attempt at 'Liar'. The line up was Gordon Edwards on piano, Theo Thunder on drums, a bass player called Billy, plus Glen Tilbrook, John Perry and an American guy called Butch, all on lead guitars. The band was named Sweet Peter by Robert Ash, after the line in 'My Redemption' – *'Sweet Peter has been and …'*

John Perry:

'We recorded "Lovers of Today" with both me and Peter playing rhythm to give it body, then I overdubbed lead and it went down in one take, mainly because we'd played it first in Manno's, then road-tested it at gigs. Producer Robert Ash was rather a laid-back presence, more engineer than producer – we were self-producing.'

John Perry admitted to Max Bell in 1978 that his guitar part is stolen from 'Heatwave' by Martha Reeves and the Vandellas. Alan Mair was delighted by the results:

'"Lovers of Today" is the perfect rock-pop song. This was the band at another level. As tight as could be, the rock and the roll. The first special track. If a song is as good as this it can't be held back.'

John Perry:

'"Peter and the Pets" was chosen for the B-side because it was always a good number live. Kellie, Alan and I always really enjoyed playing it. Comparing our version to the England's Glory version is comparing a singer/songwriter with backing to a full-blown band.'

Alan Mair was not aware of the England's Glory version when he recorded it:

'It was different from anything else that was going on at the time. So basic it almost felt childlike – just that lick with the pedalling C chord, sometimes I went from C to F to add more interest. Live, it was a song where if you didn't get the simplicity right it didn't sound good – you had to not overplay it, you had to keep it tight and basic. I loved Peter's voice on it, a bit more Lou Reedy than on other songs. When I was auditioning for Streetwalkers someone said "Does he not know that Lou Reed is still alive?" But when I heard Peter's voice properly at his house I thought it was nothing like Lou Reed.'

'Lovers of Today' photo session: Kellie, Peter, Alan and John

'Lovers of Today' was Single of the Week in all four of the UK's music weeklies – *NME*, *Sounds*, *Melody Maker* and *Record Mirror*. It came in an eccentric picture sleeve, which had been created from a cut-up gig poster. Alan Mair loved the cover:

'I look like a choir boy, John looks like he's got a hernia. I thought it really matched the music. It was Peter and Zena's creation and it was presented to us.'

'Lovers of Today' finished artwork

Album sessions

The band decamped to Escape Studios in Kent to record further tracks. (Escape was the studio used by the New York Dolls during their ill-fated visit to the UK in October 1972.) Tracks recorded here included 'Oh No', 'The Whole of the Law', 'Special View' and 'Another Girl, Another Planet'. Peter also remembers recording a downtempo version of 'Pretty Vacant'.

While at Escape, they were tracked down by Jeremy Ensor who explained that CBS were very interested in signing the band. 'Oh No' was expected to be the next single, until Ian Birch from *Melody Maker* heard a cassette copy of 'Planet' and said, 'That's the single'.

In January 1978 the backing tracks of 'No Peace For The Wicked', 'It's The Truth' and 'Someone Who Cares' were recorded at the CBS Studios in Whitfield Street. The plan was that after a hit with the uptempo 'Planet', the band would continue to confound expectations with the ballad 'Someone Who Cares', which would come to be a highlight of the band's second album.

Peter Perrett:
> 'I tried to make listening to us as difficult as possible. If you wanted to like The Only Ones you were going to have to work hard. I wanted to challenge people, so our fans would be only intelligent people with idiosyncratic tastes.'

Sandy Denny offered to do backing vocals at this stage but Peter did not take her up on the offer, despite him being a fan of early Fairport Convention.

The final recording sessions for The Only Ones were at Basing Street. John Perry admits that the piecemeal nature of recording sessions meant that the first LP lacked a discrete identity, even to the band:
> 'The choice of songs on all three studio LPs bears no relationship to when they were written, more than any other band I've been in. The first LP was never the first LP in our heads. It was more some of the songs we played that were grouped together on an LP. But we had more songs than we needed for a set so we played

live the songs we wanted to play, rather than promoting the songs on the LP. The singles were always in the set.'

Pete Makowski agrees:
'The first album represents years and years of ideas, a mishmash of songs. All the songs came from different places. It lacks unity. If an England's Glory album had came out instead of the first Only Ones album, I think more people would have got it. The Only Ones had this dichotomy where they would not have existed without the punk scene but they were great players who had it all musically but in terms of image and content they were very underground.'

Peter Perrett now regrets the approach the band took to studio work:
'We were a great live band and we just toured – we didn't pay enough attention to the studio work. We didn't really rehearse, we just went in and did it. We should have concentrated more … I thought the only worthwhile things were spontaneous and if you gave any thought to it you ruined it. That was about the only thing we had in common with punk.'

Once in the studio, the band recorded efficiently. John Perry:
'There were not many takes – one or two with the whole band playing live. Very few songs were not easy to record. If songs became hard to get we assumed it was the song's fault and they fell aside. Sometimes we'd end up keeping only the drum track and build it up again so the separation is better. "The Beast" took a lot

of takes cos it's a march in 2/4 and Kellie liked playing 4/4, it took all evening for Kellie to settle on a beat but that was unusual. We used our usual gear. Mick Taylor had also signed to CBS and he had the big room at Basing Street booked throughout the summer, he rarely turned up, leaving sixty or seventy guitars all tuned.

'Recording "The Immortal Story", I wanted a guitar with a good tremelo arm so I borrowed a couple of Taylor's and slammed those on. We were downstairs in the small room overdubbing by then. Mick Taylor was considered for a role in The Only Ones playing piano, although I hoped he would join me as twin lead guitarist. This happened while we were rehearsing at Manno's in '76. Mick was interested in Peter's songs but his American girlfriend Val wanted Mick to play with "name musicians" like Savoy Brown – very Spinal Tap!

'I would put down two or three guitar tracks and Pete and Alan would comp together the best parts – they did a great job. But with the vocals Peter took the process way too far. He took forever with his vocals. However many tracks were free he would fill up with his vocals. It took a fucking long time for him to be content with his vocals. When we had more tracks on the second LP it got worse. I could not hear any difference in any of them.'

The whole band turned up for the mixing. John Perry:
'Eight hands, everybody reaching out to turn themselves up – typical of a band's first record. I wanted to make sure the guitar was loud

enough. Every so often we reached the point where everyone had turned themselves up full so Robert would pull the faders down to zero and start again.'

The finished ten track LP lasted a mere thirty-three minutes, although as Alan Mair points out it didn't sound short because of its stylistic variety. Its brevity is even more noticeable when you consider that the LP does not include tracks released on contemporary singles.

John Perry:

'The Beatles never put their singles on their albums. Americans did, always loading LPs with singles and then a bunch of rubbish to make up the numbers. We aimed for sixteen minutes a side to get a really good cut. Peter decided on what tracks would be used. He used to lie in bed planning the first five singles. He was obsessive about the song order and the cover design. The idea was to gain attention with the first track and then you wanted a real stomper to end the side.

'People commented that it was interesting to start with "The Whole of the Law" rather than start with a thumper. We were always interested in going against prevailing wisdom. "The Beast" had to be the final track on one side or the other, a storming track to close. I looked out for making sure we didn't have adjacent songs in the same key or tempo. Peter wrote a lot of songs in D.'

A number of other songs were recorded by now but did not make the final cut. In this category John includes 'Oh

No' ('Faux Beatles lyric. Played a lot live early on'), 'In Betweens' ('Always on the A list') and 'This Ain't All It's Made Out To Be' ('put down without a definite plan – we recorded a lot of songs to see how they turned out and if they turned out well we put them on the record').

John Perry:
> 'Dave Hill from Anchor was the first to make an offer, before he set up Real. Sire were also very interested – Peter liked that he could smoke dope with MD Seymour Stein. Miles Copeland did the distribution for Vengeance so he offered us a deal. Island were very interested and label owner Chris Blackwell flew up to see us support Split Enz at Leicester University on December 3rd when we were close to signing to CBS. He said he would match any offer.'

Seymour Stein offered Peter £60,000 for his publishing.

The Only Ones signed to CBS on December 12th 1977. While the deal that Zena negotiated offered a good advance, a large part of CBS' appeal was that Peter wanted to be on the same label as Bob Dylan.

Peter now admits that he was so arrogant then that he thought it did not really matter who the band signed with, as success was inevitable. Within six months Dan Loggins, who had signed the band, left for America. His replacements were Muff Winwood and Howard Thompson, the A & R team from Island. Thus, The Only Ones were now working with the people they had turned down.

John Perry:
> 'CBS paid for the studio but they only owned the tracks we used on the record, songs that were

not used were not theirs, hence they didn't own the songs that would appear on *Remains*. The contract with CBS included us selling "Lovers of Today" to them for £1. CBS didn't come down to the studio at all. Zena would have been going up to the office periodically. By then A & R would have been Muff and Howard, who being ex-Island could just ring the engineers. "Is it going OK?" "Yes", "Are they wasting time?" "No".'

Peter Perrett:

'To begin with, CBS thought they had done really well, outbidding everyone else. CBS supremo Maurice Oberstein came to see us at home. He turned up in his Rolls Royce, complete with a uniformed young female chauffeuse and a red setter. He said: "Your first album is great and you're going to do better." He had a lot of faith in us. And we were the next big thing in the music papers for about a year, so they left us alone for the first two albums and trusted us to deliver.'

Production

John Perry:

'CBS tried to foist Sandy Pearlman on us, before he ended up doing *Give 'Em Enough Rope* for The Clash. Alan wanted Chris Thomas or his engineer Bill Price, which would have been fabulous choices but one wasn't available and we dithered and the other one went somewhere else. In the end, Peter and Alan did the production. I did more of the arrangements, before we went into the studio.'

So Alone

Peter's friendship with Johnny Thunders made him an obvious creative ally when Johnny began recording his first solo LP, *So Alone*, following the initial demise of The Heartbreakers. Together with Mike Kellie, Peter contributed to sessions held at the Island studios in St Peter's Square, Hammersmith, during March, April and May 1978. By May 2nd, Peter had provided guitar and his distinctive backing vocals to three of the best songs on the LP, 'You Can't Put Your Arms Around A Memory', 'Ask Me No Questions' and '(She's So) Untouchable'. He also played guitar on 'Subway Train' and on the title track 'So Alone'.

Mike Kellie is credited with drums on these five tracks, as well as a version of Marc Bolan's 'The Wizard'. Producer Steve Lillywhite remembers Peter and Mike as 'real gentlemen'. Other key musicians on the sessions were Paul Cook and Steve Jones from the Sex Pistols, plus the Eddie and the Hot Rods rhythm section of Paul Gray and Steve Nicol.

Peter Perrett:

'Dave Hill from Real Records was interested in Johnny Thunders doing an album but I had to promise I'd be involved. Zena negotiated a good deal for him which he totally fucked up because he just accepted a tenth of the money negotiated, just for cash. He thought he'd done really well because he had this great big bag of supposed coke but, because he wasn't a very good junkie, he didn't know what was good and what wasn't, so always got ripped off. He used drugs as an excuse for not being successful, the whole "born to lose" thing.

'I never wanted to be a loser; I couldn't see the point of losing. I used to be very competitive. At the time I didn't take it seriously but listening back to *So Alone* I'm really proud of the songs I played with [Thunders] because I think they're the best stuff he did.'

Talking to Peter Jesperson in 2017, Perrett said:

'The title track wasn't on the original album, which pissed me off because that was my favourite song. I mean, obviously, I like "Memory" and "Ask Me No Questions", but "So Alone", I liked it because it was so slow. And one of the things Johnny said to me before making the album was he felt like he had the freedom to play really slow songs. I think it was his signature album. He did some of his best work on that album. I'm proud to be a part of it.'

Interviewed by Tim Somer in 2018, Steve Lillywhite is effusive in his assessment of Perrett's involvement:

'Peter had a lot to do with it being a sane session. He was like the wise man, and I absolutely thank him for his help, because he understood Johnny more than me, because I wasn't so familiar with that lifestyle. And Peter Perrett was. So Peter, you know, would often say to me (theatrically coughs), "Johnny's on form tonight. You've gotta push him. Johnny's up, we need to get him to do a lot of work".'

This involvement is reflected on the sleeve credits: 'Produced by Johnny Thunders / Steve Lillywhite with special thanks to Steve Jones and Peter Perrett.' The

sleeve photography was done by Peter Gravelle, who had done the same job on The Only Ones debut LP.

The album was released by Real Records on October 6th 1978 to positive reviews: it remains the high-water mark in Thunders' studio career. To promote the album, The Johnny Thunders All Stars played the Lyceum on October 12th where the reception was more mixed. Peter and Kellie were All Stars for the night but sound problems and a no-show from Paul Cook and Steve Jones contributed to many fans being disappointed. Thunders sounds grumpy throughout ('I should've stayed in Queens'), although the band plays well with saxophonist John 'Irish' Earle, pianist James Honeyman-Scott and guest vocalist Patti Palladin contributing to covers of ('Give Him) A Great Big Kiss', 'Daddy Rollin' Stone' and 'These Boots Are Made for Walking'. Peter's vocals are best heard on a version of 'Memory' that replicates the studio version to good effect.

Tall Stories

Ed Hollis was manager of Eddie and the Hot Rods, who in early 1978 were doing very well commercially for Island Records. Off the back of this success, Ed proposed a singles-based label, using the best of the new wave of London musicians.

John Perry named the label Speedball and recording sessions commenced at Island's St Peter's Square studios. Island cancelled the project before any records were released, but some of the tracks eventually escaped. First up were the Heroes, (otherwise Walter Lure and Billy Rath from the Heartbreakers), plus Henri Paul Tortosa and Steve Nicol. They recorded 'Too Much Monkey/Junkie Business' (Chuck Berry) and 'Seven

Day Weekend' (Gary U.S. Bonds). In 1983 these two tracks were released as a seven-inch single by Skydog International.

Other tracks recorded for Speedball can be found on the Skydog CD, *Punks From The Underground*, also released in 1983. While misleadingly labelled ('Ed didn't want anything to do with punk' – Pete Makowski) and appallingly packaged, it is the only record of the Speedball sessions thus far. Both Heroes tracks are included, together with ten others. NME writer Nick Kent contributed two tracks, 'Chinese Shadow' and 'Switch-Hitter Dub'.

John Perry was invited to the session:
> 'Nick already had his band the Subterraneans, he is playing some basic guitar parts and I am jamming over the top of it live.'

Though the Small Faces-style instrumental 'Speedball Jive' was rumoured to be Ducks Deluxe hiding under the alias of the Speedballs, more recent research has revealed it to be John Perry and Mike Kellie.

Mike Kellie remembered the session clearly:
> 'Ed was recording Johnny Thunders in the basement. John Perry and I were there waiting for Perrett to arrive and meanwhile we got a sound and began playing.'

John Perry:
> 'It's all done on the fly. At the end you can hear the shout of "That'll do won't it?"'

A version of Cream's 'NSU' was recorded by Mike and John the same night, and this surfaced as an acetate in 2021.

The same session – Saturday 18th March 1978 – produced the high spot of the Speedball sessions, when 'Tall Stories (38 and Conscience Stricken)' was recorded by Perry, Kellie and Robert Palmer.

Mike Kellie explained:

'At some point Robert Palmer came down to say hello – he and I had been friends for a while as we were both part of the Island family – he was in Vinegar Joe while I was in Spooky Tooth. I remember we ordered a small package to lift the atmosphere, expecting a bill of around £60. When it arrived the dealer only wanted £38. Having tasted his presentation I remember clearly coining the phrase "38 and conscience stricken" to describe his actions. I remember it so clearly because I was really quite proud of the line and never forgot it.'

John Perry again:

'Kellie and I were in the studio and Palmer wandered in and picked up a bass. I just started playing a basic riff in A. What I didn't know is that Robert wrote on bass. My guitar part had lots of room for a strong bass part which we put down in a single take. Five minutes later Robert's got this lyric about "*giving me gear with the best parts missing*". It could have just been a placeholder lyric. But it fitted the song nicely and his bassline was lovely. In this instance Kellie's kit sounded glorious and he plays it straight. Completely a first take. I added a lead guitar over the top.

'I liked the records Robert Palmer had done with Little Feat but I thought they were a little bit fussy and I thought a more Free style would suit him as another avenue. Robert loved the track too, as did all the secretaries at Island, because it was a bit rougher than his usual style. I think Island would have released it under the Speedball label, with or without Robert's name, but his manager nixed it because he saw Robert as much smoother.'

John Perry's enthusiasm is totally justified. The track eventually turned up on a cassette and in 2017 was released by R'n'B Records as a seven-inch vinyl under the name PPK (Palmer, Perry, Kellie). The B-side was 'Speedball Jive', now renamed 'Kellie's Blues'.

Tall Stories single (2017, R'n'B Records)

The start of the sessions for *So Alone* coincided with the end of Speedball. John Perry was there:

'I believe Ed Hollis was due to produce *So Alone* but, at some time in the first two days of the sessions, Speedball collapsed and Lillywhite leapfrogged over Hollis to be the producer of *So Alone*. I am not sure if Ed did any sessions or whether he was lined up to do so. There were whispers about Ed being too doped, too crazy. He needed a straighter business partner. By the autumn Island had pulled the plug on Speedball. It was a summer thing, basically "What we did on our holidays". Plus someone cottoned on that Speedball was a drug reference.'

John Perry remembers that:

'when Speedball was finally stopped, Ed cleared his desk and took all the cassettes and quarter-inch tapes home. The masters would have remained at Island and would probably have got lost in the shuffle.'

Marc Zermati of Skydog eventually put the tracks from the cassettes out as *Punks From The Underground,* only missing 'Tall Stories' because he did not have the tape.

THE SONGS

THE ONLY ONES was released as CBS 82830 in May 1978 and contained ten tracks: when a CD remastered by Alan Mair was released by Sony in 2009, the 'Lovers of Today'/'Peter and the Pets' single was added, together with 'Planet' B-side, 'As My Wife Says'.

Alan Mair:
> The remastered version is so much better than the original. I remember when we were doing it I was astounded that I could suddenly hear acoustic guitars clearly and so many other aspects of the mix that just sonically aren't there in the original. And the stereo image of the remaster knocks the original out the park.

All songwriting is credited to Peter Perrett. The inner sleeve credits Peter with vocals, guitar and keyboards, John with guitar and keyboards, Alan with bass and Kellie with drums, Koulla Kakoulli (Zena's sister) is credited with backing vocals, Micky Gallagher and Gordon Edwards with keyboards, Raphael & Friends with horns. Production is assigned to The Only Ones with the assistance of Robert Ash: Robert also shares a credit for engineering with Ed Hollis, Steve Lillywhite and John Burns.

Writing in the *NME*, Nick Kent called them 'special songs'. This is what the band think of the songs that constitute their first album, *The Only Ones*, plus their views on the ones that got away.

Side One

'The Whole of the Law'

The languid opening number is a statement of intent: we are different. John Perry:

'Height of punk? Start with a ballad. I had a complete idea of how it would sound. Peter wrote it as an acoustic track without any particular idea of how he wanted it to sound. It struck me it could be done as an early Merseybeats, Fender reverb on the guitars, guitars playing the octaves. But then Alan had the idea of putting Raphael's sax over the top, which changed the track completely so not many people listening would think Merseybeats. I had a very clear idea of the descending link that opens it, more so than most things we recorded.'

The title is derived from 'Do what thou wilt shall be the whole of the Law', the modus operandi of the self-styled occultist Aleister Crowley. The name was suggested by John, who is fearsomely well read. He said:

'Peter does not read books at all but I lent him *Diary of a Drug Fiend* by Aleister Crowley. He wasn't seriously into it – "The Whole of the Law" and "The Beast" are the only songs with Crowley references. Crowley was getting a bit overdone by then so I am glad they are not too high profile. The lyric is in the tradition of songs from the 1930s, like Leadbelly's "Goodnight Irene" (*Sometimes I have a great notion to jump into the river and drown*).'

Talking about Crowley to Max Bell in 1978, Peter Perrett said:

'there are certain aspects of his behaviour I find hard to understand. But he was basically into having lots of different types of sex and taking lots of drugs and thinking of a way of making lots of money. So eventually he decided to start a religion. It's understandable – I suppose everyone wants to be God. I took "Do what thou wilt …" to refer to willpower – if you don't preserve your willpower, then you haven't got the will to love and I thought love would triumph over everything. Like everyone else I thought I was indestructible and that my willpower was so strong that I would never subjugate myself. The arrogance of youth!'

Alan Mair:

'Starting the LP with a ballad indicated that we were different to the other bands who were around at the time. I loved the lyric – so much emotion in the lyrics. The melody is bass driven so I could express myself, [engineer] John Burns made my bass more of a lead instrument. I said to the band, "how do you fancy having sax on the intro because I know this really great sax player?" I don't remember any objections, so that became a yes. I had played with Raphael in the Al Matthews Band; he had a lovely tone and came up with the intro very quickly.'

Raphael Ravenscroft was well known for having played the saxophone solo on Gerry Rafferty's hit single 'Baker Street' (February 1978). John would replace the sax solo with a guitar part when the track was played live, which it frequently was.

'The Whole of the Law' was one of the first Only Ones songs to be covered, by Yo La Tengo on their album *Painful* in 1993.

Alan Mair:
> 'The long pause at the end of "The Whole of the Law" sets up the introduction to "Planet" really well. Whenever you hear the end of "The Whole of the Law" you are listening out for the start of "Planet" – they go together.'

'Another Girl, Another Planet'

Alan Mair:
> 'Kellie said "I'm not playing that, it's a fucking punk song".'

John Perry:
> 'We'd played it a lot, it was pretty much in shape by the time we recorded it. Once the record was out it was the first song where I realised the effect of being recorded. You learn to play from records, covering other people's stuff, you strive to do it accurately. I'd had little experience of my own work being recorded. Playing "Planet" before it was released, it was wide open. Playing "Planet" once it was on a record I realised there was pressure to play it "correctly". Before you record there is an infinite set of possibilities, afterwards it's narrowed down. We always stayed pretty close to the structure of the record but

my solo always showed a little change. I'd stick close to the record but not religiously, to keep it interesting for me to play – take a few risks and see what happens.'

Alan Mair:
'I was so taken with the song I brought my cassette player to rehearsals and recorded it all. I have a whole cassette of us rehearsing it at Manno's. I was disappointed when "Planet" failed to chart. Daytime play (Radio One, Capital Radio) was limited due to the drug references being too strong. But that didn't affect band morale – we were getting great press and bigger gigs.'

The recording of 'Planet' was a saga in itself, covered in the next chapter.

'Breaking Down'

Alan Mair:
'I joined the band on August 13th 1976 and the second Tooting sessions were two weeks later. Peter didn't want to tell me that we were recording because he was going to court on a drugs charge and he might end up going to prison. So the Tooting tapes were to get something down before that happened.

'For the first three days in the studio I thought "this is so fucking weird", we were playing and it wasn't going anywhere. At the end of the third day, having recorded nothing worthwhile, we went into "Breaking Down" and the magic suddenly happened and the song had a life of its own, playing without thinking or planning. I thought "wow, that was brilliant" and I still think it's brilliant. We didn't do it live very often, if at all. Kellie was a bit tipsy, I'd had a couple of beers, maybe that is why it was so loose. It was so free, Kellie and I had never played that arrangement before. Peter did the vocal at Basing Street.'

John Perry:

'The break in the middle is trad jazz as played by Kellie at the start of his career – a good move in the middle of punk! They wanted me to play a guitar solo but I thought it was crying out for an electric piano, maybe played by Gordon Edwards. We might have played it once live – it needed to be done in concert with a seated audience not in a rock 'n' roll club.'

'City of Fun'

John Perry:

'A lot of England's Glory tracks sound to me like songwriting demos. Comparing the England's Glory and Only Ones versions shows what a good band can do. Kellie, Alan and I were all aware of the power of things like The Who, how you can generate power by arrangement. This song demonstrates what a great rhythm section we had. It had a natural Stones vibe.'

Alan Mair:

'I always wanted to do it more often live, I love the rhythm of the lyrics. I remember thinking "this is so good". Can't get Peter to do it now – something to do with the words.'

Pete Makowski's verdict:

'Alan and Kellie were the best rhythm section to come out of this nation since John Entwistle and Keith Moon.'

'The Beast'
John Perry:
'A side ender because it was a set ender. Kellie didn't like it at first because he couldn't hear a way in, so I started off playing drums as a 2/4 march (rather than 4/4 rock 'n' roll). Kellie took over and turned out one of his best performances and he ended up loving playing it. Once Kellie found a groove he was happy with, the arrangement flew together very quickly and without discussion. We never spoke. Talking about music is an appalling bore – we just played it and if I wanted to make a bit twice as long I'd just do it and then people would either play along or wouldn't. You need a certain understanding within the band, if you've got that, a good musician will catch on immediately.

'Drums and guitar are very close, a well-constructed arrangement with good parts. Rather than strumming a guitar, Peter is playing a fixed part (the intro phrase) throughout. One of the songs best arranged for two guitars – they really dovetail, I would have liked more songs like that. The break in the middle is written in short phrases rather than as a solo – motifs rather than breaks.'

Alan Mair:
'We had nine songs and I said to Peter "it feels like we need something different". He

said "I am actually writing this song, it's nearly finished, I'll bring it in tomorrow". He played the intro riff and I thought it sounded great. We had two days to go in the studio. We learnt the song in the studio, whereas all the other songs we had rehearsed heavily in advance. I loved the feel of it, the theme of the song, the brilliant lyrics, the way the song built – I fell in love with it right away. I suggested we get a brass section in to reinforce the bass chords I was playing. We used Raphael on sax and George on trombone, also from the Al Matthews Band. The brass could have been higher in the mix but other band members were not so sure about it. We finished the track on our last day of recording. The version of "The Beast" on the album is probably only the second or third time we'd played it; we didn't have time for any further takes. When we played it live I developed a stronger bass part especially on the intro.'

Sounds writer Giovanni Dadamo wrote in 1978 that:

'the reason I rate "The Beast" alongside say, "I'm Waiting for the Man", is because it uses the drug experience as a metaphor for the perennial inner and outer battle between good and evil. Hence also the vampire connection used in "The Beast".'

Peter Perrett:

'I am a very religious person in a way. I suppose I take moral stands. I do believe in good rather than evil. Both good and evil manifest themselves in such complex ways that it's difficult to tell them apart sometimes.'

Towards the end of The Only Ones when singing the song live, Peter changed the lyric of *'I know this couldn't happen to me'* **to** *'I thought this couldn't happen to me'*.

John Perry noted the significance of this:
'Yes, I noticed because the lyrics were so fixed usually. I thought OK because it's accurate. Quite an admission. Peter wrote from his own life.'

John Perry on the song's structure:
'"The Beast" was about the only place where we had room for extensive improvisation because of the outro. I always liked sixteen-bar solos – it's like saying something on a postcard rather than waffling on for twenty minutes, better to have the solo as a structured part of the song. It was always fun to play live because Kellie played it so well.'

The Greyhound, March 1977. Alan, Peter, Kellie and John

The Greyhound, March 1977. Alan, Peter, Kellie and John

The Greyhound, March 1977. Alan, Peter, Kellie and John

Side Two

'Creature of Doom'
John Perry:
> 'Comes in with a crash, so different to side one. We got bored of it quite quickly. Lesser song on record, didn't survive long in the live set after the LP was released. Songs often go and

then make a reappearance but this one went and stayed gone.'

Alan Mair:
    'Not my favourite, leaves me cold. Doesn't do for me what the other songs did. Didn't turn me on. Synth is a CS80 or Prophet 5, played by Mickey Gallagher. In retrospect, I would have replaced it with "As My Wife Says".'

'It's The Truth'

John Perry:
    'A nice mid-tempo song in D. No real arrangement, you just play and the parts came out. Bass and drums play so well it is a pleasure to play over them. There's an organ towards the end of the "y" of *memory*, thought it would be nice to bring a Hammond in late – somewhere between Garth Hudson and Billy Preston. Glissando up to the high note and the descending scale as you hold that high note – I thought it would sound great and it does.'

(Live versions that lack the organ emphasise how important it is to the song.)

John Perry:
    'A lot of good pop is 2.30 – we could have extended it but why bother? We aimed for economy throughout the LP – that's just good taste. We were experienced musicians coming from the *Rubber Soul/Revolver* era.'

Alan Mair:
    'This song grew on me. I found it slightly awkward to play at first, I had to work on it

to get a bass part I was happy with. Maybe Kellie and I weren't sitting on it properly at the beginning. We were changing the rhythm right up to the recording but I am happy with the finished version. It became a bigger song live, especially after we reformed and it has grown in stature through the years. People really love this song; it means a lot to a lot of people. On tour Peter did it acoustically when I broke a string, which I did a lot, and it worked really well.'

'Language Problem'

John Perry:

'"Language Problem" is entirely literal, written about a girl Peter met at a gig in Manchester who was spectacularly incomprehensible. The bits where he is doing gibberish are reproducing her speech. He brought her back to London and they set up in my attic for a couple of days. She went to the pub, bought a jar of pickled onions and a packet of darts and proceeded to spear the pickled onions with the darts; it's all I can remember her eating. She was the first girl that Peter had met on the road who was into dope. She snorted some and liked it and Peter liked the idea of a girl he could get high with. Zena didn't indulge in those days.'

Alan Mair:

'At rehearsals, the chord structure seemed old-fashioned to me, like "Walk Don't Run" by the Ventures. I rehearsed hard for my part, working on root notes and weaving in and out.

I liked the finished recording but not one of my favourites. Not a song we played often live.'

Peter Perrett:

'This is the song I played the most lead guitar on. John only plays lead guitar on the closing three bars. The rest is me, and the only thing I regret is that it is not twice as loud. One take and as manic as possible.'

'No Peace For The Wicked'

John Perry:

'Harmonically and rhythmically, it's a lovely piece to play. Musically a great song, highly melodic but complicated chord changes. Completely asymmetrical. Something like nine bars in the verse and seven bars in the chorus including a couple of bars of 2/4. But it makes complete sense if you follow the lyric. Though it never moves out of B major, it goes through lots of chords but no middle eight or chorus – like early Dylan with "Desolation Row". Same major scale as used in "Planet", lovely to play once you know it – I am half playing an upward figure over the vocal melody. All of which made it a disastrous choice for Richard Lloyd to play with us at the Lyceum on October 1st, 1978. The guitar solo follows the arc of the melody rather than reprising the melody. Peter's guitar is more to the fore on the outro, a part he worked out himself mathematically rather than melodically.'

Alan Mair:

'I would play this song to other people to illustrate what I was up to with The Only Ones

– fantastic song, chords weaving in and out. Reminded me of "Lovers of Today" because of its unusual structure. I love the choice of the chords and Peter's voice. Great lyrics, that's how Peter lived most of the time. The lyric is kind of a forerunner to Morrissey, he must have listened to that closely. Very proud of that song.'

Johnny Marr was certainly a regular visitor to The Only Ones dressing room when they played anywhere near Manchester.

Peter Perrett, talking to Thomas H Green again:

'It is tongue-in-cheek because back then I was really happy, really content and enjoying my life. I never used to take things that seriously. Back then I didn't give a fuck. The music I did in the seventies in The Only Ones, most of it was humorous. Gallows humour maybe, talking about things that on the surface might have been bad situations. But I didn't used to invest too much emotional depth in them, I used to try and laugh. Now I sort of feel guilty about some of the things I did, talking about relationships …'

'The Immortal Story'

Peter Perrett:

'I named it after an Orson Welles film which is about a similar subject; when success and money give you a certain amount of power and that's a dangerous thing. I was enjoying being successful and having people do things for me. That was changing me as a human being. In a way that's why, when the band broke up, I found it easier not to have anything to do with the music business. I always thought it was more important to be a human being first and a musician second.'

John Perry:

'Peter is more knowledgeable about films than literature and films are a brilliant source of titles for any songwriter, for example *River of No Return* or *The Big Sleep*. As a number, I thought it never quite came off, a little bit of a mess. Almost a single chord thrash in A with Marriott / Townsend chords. Its 4/4 but changes when the horns appear. Kellie's playing a straight march 2/4 (one/two, left/right) – but the instruments play 5/4 which gives the effect of things getting out of step. Medium fun song to play live. I borrowed Mick Taylor's guitars for this as I needed a tremelo arm for the horse whinnies. The vocal part is doubled, conceived as Peter conversing with himself. Other places he sings a harmony. Peter wanted the song to get more and more manic and end with an explosion like "7 and 7 Is". It gave me the opportunity to cut loose live but not over anything particularly interesting – it would have been more interesting to improvise over "No Peace For The Wicked" because of greater harmonic opportunities.'

Alan Mair:

'Great song to play live, in the same way as "The Beast". After the intricacy of "No Peace For The Wicked", it's great to rock out. We tried a brass section but it felt too much like "The Beast" so we just kept the sax. We wanted a big ending like "All You Need Is Love" so we added a load of explosions and a crescendo. It could do with an alternative vocal mix: having vocals left and right didn't really work, maybe would have been better as a straight double-tracked vocal.'

The B-sides
John Perry:
'As a record buyer I'd always liked singles. Nice to have good B-sides. Something interesting or funny, where people had paid a little bit of extra attention, for example the Stones with "The Under Assistant West Coast Promotion Man", and "Spider and the Fly".'

'Special View' (aka 'Telescopic Love')
B-side to 'Another Girl, Another Planet', CBS 6228, released April 14th 1978.
John Perry:
'Meant to be a spoof of all these white bands playing very bad reggae – this is more calypso/one drop. The Kinks always did calypsos like "Apeman". We recorded two versions of "Special View" – a reggaeish version and also a semi-acoustic version, which I prefer.'
Alan Mair:
'Peter and I thought "let's try and do something that's not just drum kit based". So we played a sort of calypso on the drum cases, miked up, similar to what Lindsey Buckingham would do on "Tusk". Kellie wasn't playing, he was just looking at us and feeling insulted we didn't want his drum kit. He joined in eventually, probably

playing the kettle. The lyrics are brilliant, I loved the humour.'

Peter Perrett:
'We recorded a pipe organ part at Basing Street which was really sweet but then left it off the version we released.'

'As My Wife Says'

B-side to 'Another Girl, Another Planet', CBS 6576, released August 18th 1978.

John Perry:
'Peter conceived it as a bit of a throw away song. He had a more straightforward strummed version but I had a riff for it. Great song. Peter judges songs mainly by the lyric. Underrated and underused, it would have fleshed out the LP nicely. A song I always liked – good lyric, started off with a strum through a straightforward chord sequence and we recorded it like that. Then I thought of the guitar riff that runs all the way through, the later and better version which doubles up the G and introduces a drone.'

(The latter arrangement is best heard on the live version that opens Jungle Record's LP, *The Big Sleep*.**)**

Alan Mair:
'I love the song – the lyric grabs me. The recorded version lacks the brilliant guitar riff that John added later. Fantastic live song albeit very short. But no one ever said "That's short" because the song said everything it needed to.'

'ANOTHER GIRL, ANOTHER PLANET'

'ANOTHER GIRL, ANOTHER PLANET' continues to have an impact out of all proportion to its lack of commercial success. Having failed to chart twice in 1978, the track's first UK chart appearance was in January 1992 when, as a single with the Psychedelic Furs' 'Pretty in Pink', it spent two weeks in the UK charts, peaking at 57.

Contrary to popular opinion, the song's primary inspiration was not drugs but love, as Peter Perrett explains:

'It would have been about April '77, because we had it recorded by June. It was inspired by this girl from Yugoslavia. I didn't go out with her, but she was like a total space cadet, which when I was really young I found interesting. She was just a bit weird – she'd say crazy things, and it just got me thinking that every girl has something different to offer.

'It would have been written on my Guild acoustic. I think any good song should sound all right on an acoustic guitar. It's not about heroin. I mean, I'd started experimenting with heroin at that time – I was probably on it about once a month – but I didn't think of myself as a junkie until 1980 or '81, after the band broke up. I always enjoyed writing ambiguous lyrics that could be taken on two or three different levels. You know, it's like "Love Is The Drug" or "Addicted To Love". I put in drug-related imagery, but it wasn't about drugs. At that time I was more addicted to sex and infatuation than I was to drugs.'

'Planet' was recorded at John 'Johnnie' Burns' Escape Studio facility in Kent during the summer of 1977. John Perry's diary for August 1977 records two periods at Escape, Friday 19th–Sunday 21st and Bank Holiday Monday and Tuesday, 29th and 30th. John Burns was a former college classmate of Andy Johns, who was then the chief engineer at Morgan Studios. All of Island's recordings were handled by Morgan and it was where Burns cut his musical teeth, assisting on sessions with Humble Pie, Jethro Tull, Blodwyn Pig, Ten Years After, Donovan, King Crimson and Spooky Tooth.

Alan Mair explains:

'Johnnie had been recommended to us as a really good guy, a great guy and very switched-on, and since we wanted to record outside of London, Escape seemed a logical place to go.'

Award-winning journalist and author Richard Buskin conducted an extensive interview with Alan Mair and John Burns about the recording of 'Planet', which formed the basis of a fascinating article that appeared in *Sound On Sound* magazine.

Alan Mair first heard 'Planet' when Perrett played it on guitar during pre-Escape rehearsals at Manno's studios on the King's Road and, he told Buskin, he was:

'just blown away. It was more or less complete, with maybe one or two lines of lyrics to fill in, and it also didn't have the long intro. That was created by the band. The basic format of the song was all there – the chords, verses and chorus – and, as with all of Peter's material, we worked through it until everything fitted … when we got to *Escape* we didn't think, "right, let's get the tape ready, let's roll". We would just play until we felt comfortable, and then, without telling the other guys in the band that we were about to record, I would nod at John to kind of say, "we're going to play for serious now".

'John's a master at that. I mean, there's nothing worse than doing a song and then turning to the engineer and saying "Did you get that?" only to find out it's gone. I'm a great believer in magic happening occasionally. On the first day it was kind of obvious that we were just talking and playing little bits of the song, but after that I gave John the nod, and when Peter started I spontaneously came in with the bass on the offbeat. I don't know where that inspiration came from, because on all of the rehearsal tapes I was playing on the downbeat. In this case, however, I came in on the offbeat and I thought "Yeah".

'I kind of nodded at Kellie to make sure he wasn't just watching us without intending to come in on drums, thinking that we were running through it without doing a full take. So Kellie came in and then John came in, and more or less that whole introductory guitar part was done straight off. The entire song went beautifully after that, and it crystallised into a much more powerful version than we'd played before.'

Then John Perry did his bit. Writing on MySpace he said:

> 'While it was still warm I overdubbed the lead. I knew the shape, the form of the guitar solo and the intro. I knew it would start low and work upwards, but I hadn't settled on completed phrases. Where you're stacking up guitars it's good to vary the timbre by using different amps. Usually that means grabbing whatever's lying round the studio. In a corner I found a Marshall Stack with *Jeff Beck* stencilled on the side. I thought "hmm, okay. Jeff Beck eh? Let's see about that …" Plugged in, put on the cans and bashed out some lead. Put the guitar down, wandered back into the control room to ask how the amp was sounding. "How was that? Shall I try one?" And they're all jumping up and down in their chairs. Why are they laughing? A chorus of Alan, Peter, Kellie and Burns all going "no … no …no …THAT'S IT! Don't touch it!".'

John Perry continued:

> '"OK" I thought, it's always gratifying to knock off work early and put your feet up but I didn't think we'd started. Wasn't even sure we'd been recording. Musicians and songwriters are really not the best editors of their own work – you really can't be both sides of the glass at once. They play it back and it does sound pretty good so – having it done it on a Strat' or a Tele – I thought I'd double it with the Les Paul Junior, fatten it out, give it some body. This worked fine on the intro but the extra guitar wasn't needed on the break.'

At this stage, The Only Ones simply thought they'd made a great demo of 'Another Girl, Another Planet' and departed Escape with a cassette copy of this and the other tracks committed to tape. After all, once they signed a record deal they would have the money to pay for a bigger, better equipped studio that, they assumed, would enable them to make a bigger, better sounding record. And so it was that, the following year, sessions commenced at Basing Street, again with engineer Robert Ash.

Alan Mair told Richard Buskin:

'We continued recording "Planet" and did several different versions, in between working on other songs. At the end of the day, we probably had three takes to work with, but I remember sitting there, thinking, "These just don't feel right." I told the guys in the band: "This isn't as good as the demo. We haven't captured that magic." It didn't jump out of the speakers in the same way. There was no spark. When I brought the cassette in and played it, everyone agreed. We'd hit that point, and I believe you only achieve that magic once.'

John Burns said:

'It's all about atmosphere. We did fart around and have some fun. If you're recording, it shouldn't be too damned serious, and The Only Ones were a pleasure to work with. The whole thing was simple; two guitars, bass, drums and vocals. Bang-bang. It was easy, and so you could muck around with effects and have a bit of a laugh.'

Indeed, one effect that The Only Ones didn't know how to recreate, along with the aforementioned magic, was some juddering feedback on the drums at the start of the track, created by John Burns:

> 'I was always doing things like that. I fed the drums back on themselves, routing the toms' signal from the playback head onto the sync head. Obviously, I didn't put it through the headphones, because otherwise Mike would have said, "What the hell's going on?", but when the guys heard it in the control room they all thought it was great. It just happened to be on that take, and I probably put it on a separate track just in case it ended up being the actual master and this might screw it up.'

Alan Mair decided they would have to get hold of the sixteen-track, transfer it to twenty-four-track and then see if they could develop things from there. Not that this turned out to be straightforward either. He said:

> 'We sent the roadies to pick up the sixteen-track tape and bring it back to Basing Street, but it wouldn't play on the machine they had there and everything sounded muffled. Obviously, the heads were aligned differently to those on Johnnie's machine, and no matter how much we fiddled about we couldn't get it to sound right. In a moment of desperation we told the roadies, "You're gonna have to go back to Escape and pick up the sixteen-track machine". They went "Oh, fucking hell, Alan", and we said "No, look, this is really important". So off they went, back down to Johnnie, and Johnnie was like, "You're not bloody taking my

machine away! What, on the back of your van? Sod off, you must be joking!".

They weren't, but John Burns knew what he was talking about; not only was the machine expensive, but its head alignment would be thrown out of whack anyway, following a bumpy ride from Kent to London. Alan Mair:

'He called me and said, "Alan, all I need to do is a tone tape for you. Trust me, it'll be OK". I said, "C'mon, Johnnie, let them take the machine," but he insisted: "I'll put some tones onto a tape and then the engineers can realign the machine in Basing Street".'

Which is what happened.

Alan Mair:

'It felt like an eternity but when they put the sixteen-track on, there in all its glory was "Planet", pounding out of the speakers, and it was like heaven. It just sounded fantastic. A complete performance with no splices; pure rock and roll, from the first note to the last. And then, when we did the transfer to twenty-four-track, that gave us eight tracks to make some additions. First off, Peter did a proper vocal, because we knew what he'd done was just a guide and since he hadn't been spot-on the mike all the time, it needed improving. Other than that, there were a couple of double-tracked vocal parts on the chorus, a second guitar on the intro and solo and at that point we decided, OK, we've got the master, now let's start mixing.

'Peter and I were very hands-on, so Robert Ash set up a mix session, the whole band was there, and I said, "Because of the way it was recorded, we just can't get any separation between the bass drum and snare. That means we can't get the bass drum totally on its own to compress it and do what we want, we can't get the snare drum on its own, and so we're really handicapped in terms of getting the drums to sound powerful enough". Kellie to my astonishment just said, "Oh, I'll put another kit on top of it". I said, "You can do that?" and he said, "Yeah." I said, "What, matching the drum breaks, the tempo and all the tiny variations?" He said, "Sure." I said, "But can you even remember every break that you played?" We were talking about a recording that had been made about six months earlier. He said "Yeah, no problem", and so I said, "OK then, let's go for it."

'We were only at Basing Street for two weeks, working on that first album, and everything was set up for the recording of the other tracks, and so Kellie sat down at his kit and off he went, and within a few seconds we were all looking at each other like "Bloody hell!". It was spot-on. Then about three-quarters of the way through, there was a little click of his sticks and he kind of lost his feel. Our hearts just sank. We all went "Oh, no! Kellie, that was perfect … " and he just went "It's OK, I'll do it again." I was looking at him like, "I can't believe this" but then he did a second take and it was absolutely bloody perfect: his own kit on top of his kit, not the tiniest bit of phasing, nothing. I said, "Kellie, that's blown me away. What you've just done is absolutely phenomenal." And that's how rock-solid Mike Kellie is.'

Mike Kellie was more circumspect:

'I do remember everybody being quite flabbergasted, but I don't remember the actual thought process. I just did it. It had to be done. I was always astounded that it was so impressive. The easiest person to play with has to be yourself.'

Alan Mair:

'When you listen to "Planet", you're actually hearing two kits. Not only was the ambience of the first kit an integral part of the sound, but to get the feel there was obviously no way he could just play the bass drum and the snare. With the two kits on separate tracks, the new kit was at the front insofar as the snare and the bass drum, while the crash cymbals and other bits and pieces were at an equal volume, but we certainly didn't pull the other kit back or submerge its ambience, as there was natural overspill from the bass and guitars recorded at Escape. If we'd have taken the first kit out we'd have lost part of the dynamics. What's more, that kit also had the backwards reverb at the start. The point was, we now had a very clear bass drum and a very clear snare drum to do a really good mix. When I think about what Kellie did, it still sends chills up my spine. That's what saved the track, because if we hadn't added the second kit I don't think it could have been released.'

One more part remained to be added, as John Perry wrote on MySpace:

'A few days later, Peter turns up at my place off the Fulham Road, very excited and obviously been up all night. "Listen to this," he says. He'd run into Ed Hollis after our gig at the Rock Garden and together with Ed's tape op Steve Lillywhite they'd gone back to Island studios in St. Peter's Square and worked on "Planet". Peter couldn't contain himself. He was shuffling, drumming on his knees. Ed Hollis was the greatest producer in the history of rock and roll, and so on, and so on. Then he played the cassette. It had a sort of excitement but it was shrill beyond belief. Brittle. All cocaine treble and fingernails down the blackboard high frequencies. Unusable. But it did have one new component. Peter had done a new lead vocal in single take. The mix was rejected by all, but the vocal stayed.'

The Rock Garden, Covent Garden, 5 April 1977. Alan, Kellie, Peter and John.

'Planet' legacy

Talking to Thomas H.Green in 2015 Peter Perrett said:

'At one time I resented having to do "Planet" at every gig – there was one gig where I didn't do it and people complained. At some gigs in the '90s, I used to start with it to get it out of the way! But as I got older, I appreciated that it's better to have one song like that than not have any songs that get across to a large audience. If people discover the best of my work through that one song, then great. When I played with my next band, The One, I didn't want to be a nostalgic act. Some promoters insisted on putting "featuring Peter Perret" on posters and when the album came out it mentioned Peter Perrett on it, but I wanted to start again.

'At gigs I started off doing a third Only Ones stuff, two-thirds new stuff. I hadn't played for fifteen years so I had to pander to the audience a little bit. I remember doing a gig where I didn't play "Planet". A famous Irish comedian was there. I can't remember his name but it was the first time he'd seen me. We spoke afterwards and I thought, "Maybe I'm being a bit selfish not playing it". If I went to see someone live I'd want to hear songs I loved. After that I played "Planet". I've got to play it every gig but it's not a song I really enjoy singing, especially now I'm older, because it's quite fast and takes a lot out of you to do it with any energy. It's one of the least comfortable songs to sing so, from that point of view, a burden. But I'm really grateful to it because lots of people I respect have done versions, like R.E.M. Hearing iconic voices singing it is a compliment. It makes me appreciate there was something special about the band. The Cure's version is good. I don't think it's the best song I've written. The band played great and it's really exciting. It encapsulated the energy of the time. It means a lot to people who were around, an iconic single that was always popping up in John Peel's *Festive 50* in the early '80s.'

The song was placed at number eighteen in the *All Time Festive 50* millennium edition: when playing it in 1980's Festive Fifty, Peel introduced it as an 'artful little caprice'.

Versions

JOHN PERRY DESCRIBES 'Planet' as 'having a simple enough structure that any teenage band can thrash it out' and many have. The first released version appears to be by Greg Kihn in 1986. Other covers include those by The Lightning Seeds, Blink-182, Pete Doherty and the Libertines, The Coal Porters, The Nutley Brass, Belle and Sebastian, The Ukulele Orchestra of Great Britain, Misty Miller, Johnny Thunders and The Cure (a soundcheck in Pittsburgh, August 1987).

The song's title was used as the name of a 1992 American independent movie directed by Michael Almeryda, although the song itself does not appear in the film. 'Planet' does feature in two UK movies: *That Summer* (1979) and *Me Without You* (2001). It also appears in *Different For Girls* (1996), *Dirty Weekend* (1993) and *Blue Iguana* (2018), as well as on the soundtrack of *D.E.B.S* (2004) and *Get Him To The Greek* (2010). Gregg Mottola's science-fiction comedy *Paul* (2011) uses 'Planet' in the opening scene. The 2018 film *Her Smell* features Elizabeth Moss as 'Becky Something', a Courtney Love-style grunge rock singer who delivers a surprisingly effective version of 'Planet' early on in the film.

The Replacements carried a torch for this song the longest; it is their most frequently played cover version. They were introduced to the song by manager and ex-record store owner Peter Jesperson. The earliest recorded instance of them covering 'Planet' is a gig in Madison in January 1984 and it was a regular live staple until they split in 1991. A version recorded live at the University of Wisconsin in Milwaukee in June 1989 was given away as a free flexi-disc with issue number forty of *The Bob* magazine. The whole gig, including 'Planet', was finally released as part of the *Dead Man's Pop* box set in 2019. 'Mats front man Paul Westerberg carried on playing 'Planet' in his solo shows. When the Replacements reunited and played the London Roundhouse on June 2, 2015, they included 'Planet' as the last song of the night. In July 2017, Peter Perrett and John Perry joined 'Mats bass player Tommy Stinson and his band Bash & Pop onstage in London for a good-natured, if rather over-populated, version of 'Planet', after which Tommy thanked them, saying 'that meant the world to me'.

In his 1993 book *Rock and Roll: The 100 Best Singles*, veteran rock writer Paul Williams uses the account of how he heard 'Planet' for the first time to show how fantastic music is always around, waiting to be discovered:

'So here's to the guy with the Brooklyn accent in a pub in Manchester in 1990 who not only told me about this song but pulled a CD player and an assortment of his favourite CDs out of his travel bag and initiated me on the spot. It's the sort of single which, if you'd heard it out of the blue, you'd call the radio station right away to get the name of the artist, and you wouldn't be surprised to find it #1 in the world six weeks later. Yeah well, sometimes lightning strikes and sometimes it misses. But oh what a perfect record.'

The company that 'Planet' keeps in Paul's book includes 'Honky Tonk Women', 'Roadrunner', 'All Along the Watchtower' and 'I Can See For Miles'.

The song reached a whole new audience when used to soundtrack a Vodafone TV advert in 2006, although The Only Ones original was subsequently replaced over Christmas by a more seasonal cover version by Bell X1. Earlier attempts by IKEA and American Express to use 'Planet' to soundtrack their TV commercials had foundered over Peter's inability to give his consent. On the back of the Vodafone tie-up, Alan Mair persuaded the other three members of the band to return to live work – John Perry maintaining it could not be a reformation as they had never officially split up. The initial performance at the All Tomorrows Parties festival was so well received that a string of live dates followed, in the UK and abroad. Recording sessions were less successful and the band ceased activities with Mike Kellie's death in 2017. At the time of writing, the last time that Alan, Peter and John played 'Planet' together was at the Somerstown Festival in Kings Cross on July 13th 2019.

Alan Mair said:

'At the time I didn't think "Planet" overshadowed the other songs on the LP ("The Beast" was my favourite song to play). It was obvious it was going to be a single. As time has gone on it has overshadowed the other material. Because "Planet" was not a hit, people discover it for themselves which gives it longevity. Young people continue to discover The Only Ones. The fact that it was not a hit makes it more iconic.'

AND THEN …

The Sleeve

THE SLEEVE ART was a 'rush job' and it shows, according to the photographer responsible, Peter Gravelle, aka Peter Kodick:

'Looking back at the LP design now I don't particularly like it. I don't mind the front cover. But the back cover looks like some old rock band. The inside picture is OK but printed on absolute shit paper.'

A fashion and advertising photographer, Gravelle took on The Only Ones cover shoot on the back of finishing an international campaign for St Moritz cigarettes:

'I didn't hang out with bands – I don't even really like bands. In 1976 the work snowballed because every record company signed their own token punk band and wanted a punk photographer to do the pictures so I fulfilled that role. Having done the cover for *Damned Damned Damned*, Jake Riviera came up with my new name of "Peter Kodick". John Perry was a friend of mine, so they [The Only Ones] asked me to do their record cover. I did the front cover, the back cover, the inside pic of the band sitting down but not the live shots. Nothing was really planned and it was a rush job … We shot it in the evening – not the best time to do it. No make up or hairdressers or stylists like you get today.'

Peter Perrett remembers:

'The back cover was shot on the stairs at Basing Street. The front cover was at the top of the stairs – two shots, double exposure. One in front of a wall of glass, the other behind the wall, I think the whole thing took ten minutes in a break from recording. Easiest £1,000 Pete ever made! I was into "ripping off the corporations", never crossed my mind we paid for everything in the end.'

John Perry was similarly unmoved:

'We'd been reminded to bring some extra clothes but otherwise it was just a tea break in a regular Basing Street evening.'

Commercial photographer Lawrence Impey, who had photographed the band live at the Speakeasy and Manno's (he'd known Peter Perrett since 1974 – once again the connection was a mutual love of Bob Dylan) was equally underwhelmed by the cover:

'It is some sort of double exposure or double printing but I see no virtue in it. I am seeing bad lighting, a direct flash. Lighting is coming from underneath, which you want to avoid. The back cover shot is bad as well.'

Peter Gravelle says the front cover double exposure was deliberate. He also investigated using a fisheye lens that made the band look like they were reflected in a

puddle. The challenge for him was how to represent The Only Ones:

> 'My big thing is for the first LP you should see four people on the cover … it's difficult because there's always the good looking one, the one who's not so bad, the one who really sticks out. The thing with The Only Ones is you have four very different characters.'

Peter Perret was one who really stuck out, with 'an interesting face and an interesting look' and Gravelle toyed with putting him alone on the front, 'with a group shot on the back.' But this caused problems with the logistics of the band – 'so now is it Peter Perrett and The Only Ones?'

Peter Gravelle:

> 'I did the lettering on the front cover and handed it into the CBS art department, they must have put together the back cover and the insert. The bright colours for the title lettering were to stand out from the background without having to make the picture smaller and have the title separately. I used a Times Roman font that I'd used on the embossed Snatch single cover. I also did the single cover with flowers for "Planet". We probably all looked at the pictures on a light box and agreed on the front cover. All the films went to CBS, as I don't have any pictures in my files. They dumped everything in the garbage about ten years later.'

He stopped doing band photography because:

> 'they came to you because they were stuck, they'd tried other things and came to you as a last resort, so they need it yesterday and the record's coming out tomorrow.'

The black and white picture used inside the sleeve was taken after a gig at The Marquee on March 13th. Light In The Attic records announced a limited edition rerelease of *The Only Ones*, with a gatefold sleeve, in November 2020, but this has seemingly yet to appear.

Peter Gravelle's alternative ideas for The Only Ones front cover

Promoting the LP

THOUGH CBS CERTAINLY spent money promoting *The Only Ones*, it was generally invested in a clueless manner. Max Bell at the *NME* – an early staunch supporter of The Only Ones – was:

> 'somewhat bewildered by the artistic marketing with which CBS have lumbered the group. Firstly, the album cover was an idea that failed to work except as some half-assed trippy Floyd joke. This was followed by a spate of advertising where one might have thought the artefact under promotion was a collection of fishing songs.'

A *Radio One In Concert* recording, transmitted on July 5th, saw The Only Ones share the billing with hard rockers Whitesnake; a revealing juxtaposition of the old and the new. Over thirty minutes, the songs played were 'The Beast', 'The Immortal Story', 'Lovers of Today', 'Someone Who Cares', 'Another Girl, Another Planet', 'Flowers Die' and 'She Says' (an early version of 'No Solution'). It is likely that the set started with 'The Immortal Story' and finished with 'The Beast'. Out of seven songs, only three came from the LP the band were allegedly promoting. Like all of The Only Ones' BBC appearances, the songs were played with great verve. Listening to how good 'Flowers Die' sounds here makes its non-appearance on any of the band's studio LPs inexplicable.

Another promotional appearance was playing 'Another Girl, Another Planet' on Associated Television's *Revolver* programme on September 2nd. Introduced by a typically sardonic Peter Cook as 'proof there is unintelligent life on other planets', the video is cleverly edited in the style of a 1950s sci-fi cartoon, with the band playing live in front of an enthusiastically pogoing teen audience.

Faster Than Lightning

THERE IS VERY little live footage of the band from this period. Video exists of a 1979 gig in Minneapolis but synchronising a soundtrack has proved challenging. In 1991, the growing demand for a visual record of the band led to a deal with Virgin Vision to release *Faster Than Lightning*, a one-hour VHS of The Only Ones in their prime. Clips of the band's performances were interspersed with Peter being interviewed in Forest Hill by Henry Williams. The footage was released as a DVD on the band's own OneVision label in 2008.

'Lovers of Today' is the single version, filmed at the Speakeasy in April 1977 for a French production company. It shows the band with longish hair but otherwise fully formed. Everyone looks more carefully coiffed by the spring 1978 CBS promo film for 'Planet', although John's white shoes, white jacket and mirrored aviators give him a south London gangster vibe. Filmed on a large stage, Peter is, for some reason, standing stage left in Alan's usual position.

CBS succeeded in getting the band on BBC 2's *The Old Grey Whistle Test* on June 13th to play live versions of 'No Peace For The Wicked' and 'The Beast': the DVD omits the latter, possibly as licensing material from the

BBC is notoriously expensive. By now, Peter, Alan and John were all wearing white shoes: Peter took a leaf out of the Keith Richards style book and wore a woman's top, delicate in white lace.

A playback version of 'Planet' done for Irish TV station RTE is notable for John wearing an Irish farmer's green tweed suit and matching tank top. By the time they played 'The Beast' live for RTBF Belgium pop show *Follies* in May 1979, the band was looking more stylish – John all in black and Peter in voluminous white trousers with a black lace top. The lyrics had changed to a prophetic '*I never thought it could happen to me*'. A live version of 'Planet' sparkles. Finally, there are four tracks from a November 1979 gig at The Paradiso, Amsterdam. Shot for Dutch cable TV station VPRO, the cameraman's position at the side of the stage means we see a lot of Peter, some of Alan but little of John or Kellie. Stage lighting gives the picture a ghoulish green quality but it remains the only extant footage of a live gig from this era and the version of 'The Immortal Story' is ferocious.

In 1993, Jungle released fourteen tracks from the same gig on CD as *The Big Sleep*, with excellent sound and performances throughout.

Reviews at the time

Giovanni Dadamo, *Sounds:*
 '*The Only Ones* is a superb album. Can you say "very superb"?'

Nick Kent, *NME*:
'There is a compelling self-confidence behind The Only Ones' vision which attracted me from the outset, this starting with Peter Perrett's haunting songs and brazenly unorthodox singing, and stretching through to the resolve and unity of the players themselves.'

Ian Birch, Melody Maker:
'I rate The Only Ones as one of the most stimulating and original bands around. That word "original" has been sorely taxed of late but if ever its application was justifiable, it is here and now.'

Robert Christgau, *Village Voice*:
'Dry witty and unassumingly polysyllabic, his sentiment sheathed in irony, Peter Perrett is a bemused/distressed/displaced romantic with an uncanny command of conventional hard rock – like a nice Lou Reed, or Ray Davies gone to college. Which means he's a new waver by historical association ... an artist who may be major if he sticks at it.'

Reviews in retrospect

Rod Little, The Only Ones re-release sleeve notes 2009:
'The Only Ones were the best British rock band of the 1970s, and maybe since ... No band merged the good things about the dubious and over-hyped form, rock music, than this disparate collection of sometimes querulous individuals

who coalesced in south London in the mid-1970s when the first glimpse of punk were showing beneath the hem of rock's increasingly ludicrous outer-garments. They were too clever, too literate to be punks, too acidic to be hippies and too disillusioned with what rock had become to be the conventional Brit hard rock band. There was a grace and rather fragile beauty about their music which separated them from everything around.'

Colin Larkin, *All Time Top 1000 Albums*, **Guinness Publishing 2004:**

'The Only Ones were the closest thing the UK had to Johnny Thunder's Heartbreakers, a laconic shamble of a band who were, at moments, touched by a creative greatness that made you get out of the glare.'

Mark Deming, www.allmusic.com:

'Perrett's tales of one guy's search for love and coherence in a fractured world are intelligent, witty and deeply cutting at all times. If the creative ambitions of The Only Ones sometimes comes at the price of a tight stylistic focus that would make these songs cohere better, every track is memorable in its own way, and these ten songs always have heart, soul and honesty to spare – and if that isn't always the benchmark of punk rock, it's at least in the neighbourhood.'

Shiffi Le Soy, www.headheritage.co.uk:

'Scandalously ignored by the record-buying public after thirty odd years this bona fide classic remains one of my favourite LPs. For one brief moment The Only Ones debut shone brightly and gave us thirty-five minutes of perfect, twisted pop. Describing the search for love and meaning in a nether world of narcotic romanticism, it's an album of intelligence, wit and emotional honesty which also happens to rock like a mutha. And thirty years later it continues to shine on, a timeless jewel which only improves with age.'

EPILOGUE

JOHN PERRY:

'Punk is not a fair characterisation of The Only Ones' sound. I would say we were a mainstream rock 'n' roll band in the style of The Who and The Stones. Peter was very keen on Lou Reed, I was very keen on Jonathan Richman so it was a kind of crossover between them. If you are doing something good and something genuinely original when you start out nobody in the press knows how to categorise it. If it's easy to pigeonhole it'll probably be easy to sell but it probably isn't that original. Whenever you do something that the press is having a genuine problem figuring out, you're probably onto something.'

Peter Perrett:

'I don't really listen to my old stuff. If I had to make the first LP again I'd probably make the same choices and the same mistakes. It was different to what was around then, even the stupid cover with the double exposure and echoes of the first Pink Floyd LP. Everyone else was being photographed in moody black and white on bomb sites in Camden. I paid a lot of attention to the music but not the sleeve which I saw as packaging around a product.'

Listening to *The Only Ones* today I am taken straight back to my late teens and early twenties, which as for most people were times of immense confusion. I had been kicked out of college – it turns out you can't study for exams in the back of a Ford Transit. I was back in suburbia, living with my parents with few prospects and a complicated emotional life which nobody understood, least of all me. *The Only Ones* made an appropriate soundtrack to those troubled times and was a source of great comfort.

Forty-plus years later, *The Only Ones* is still a great listen but my relationship to music has changed. Music is less magical these days. I know more about the music industry, about how the process of recording works. I understand that inter-band relationships rarely resemble the Monkees' shared house. I have realised that for most working musicians the big-name recording contract is a relatively brief part of their career. Thanks to The Only Ones return to perform a lap of honour in 2007, I was able to meet and hang out with the band, especially John and Alan who turned out to be great company with a good sense of perspective of what The Only Ones achieved. Kellie I knew less well. Peter has remained more distant, but I don't blame him for being wary of writers when many only want to talk about drugs rather than music.

Looking back at The Class of '76, it is hard to make the case for the Great Punk LP. The music that was igniting London during 1976 and early 1977 was best experienced live in sweaty clubs and on seven-inch vinyl. There were swathes of great singles from the first wave such as The Clash, The Sex Pistols, The Saints, The Boys, The Damned and The Buzzcocks. But LPs? Not so much. The best tracks on The Sex Pistols' only real LP had all been released as singles and the debut Clash LP suffered from underproduction and an uninspiring drummer – two common punk problems. The Clash upped their game by recruiting Topper Headon (drums) and Guy Stevens (production) and became an exhilarating live act. In late 1979 they recorded the *London Calling* album, a double LP that for once justified its length.

The Heartbreakers live were certainly a match for the sass of The Only Ones, partly due to the power and drive of ex-Dolls drummer Jerry Nolan. However a mastering fault neutered the sound of their 1977 debut LP *LAMF*, and the world would not hear what it had missed until Jungle released a revised version in 2021. What *LAMF* and *London Calling* shared with *The Only Ones* was great playing, distinctive songwriting, economical arrangements, an absence of pretence and a sense of exhilaration at what rock 'n' roll could still achieve.

When The Only Ones ceased playing the first time, I shared the frustration of *Melody Maker* editor Steve Sutherland over the band's lack of commercial success. His review of their goodbye-for-now gig on March 8th 1981 at the Lyceum ends:

> 'suffice to say anyone out there who never bought an Only Ones record is directly responsible for the death of one of Britain's best-ever bands and, personally, I'll never forgive you.'

Now I think they did all they could.

As John Perry said to Nina Antonia in *The One and Only* (1996):

> 'Peter is always very keen on citing drugs as the problem which led to The Only Ones break up, which is nonsense. The major cause of the break up was maladministration. Plenty of people keep an efficient organisation going through far more involved drug usage than we had. Drugs are a convenient catch-all excuse to blame for a whole variety of stuff. In my view, the whole time the band was going, it [drugs] made Peter a bit late for setting off to gigs sometimes but we rarely missed any gigs. I turned up on time and stayed in tune, and, beyond that, my view was that my personal life was my own. People's fundamental natures don't change. Above a certain level of disorganisation there is no cure.'

The indolence that Nick Kent noted in his first encounter with the band was arguably more significant than drug use. A useful comparison is the career trajectory of The Pretenders. Although they formed slightly later than The Only Ones (March 1978), founder Chrissie Hynde had been part of the same musical scene. Prior to The Pretenders, Chrissie had been involved with various ill-judged McLaren and Westwood musical ventures. She appears on *So Alone* and Pretenders' guitarist James Honeyman-Scott was part of Johnny Thunders' Allstars. The Pretenders signed to Real Records, who had earlier attempted to sign The Only Ones. Like Perrett, Hynde was arresting visually, she looked great onstage, sang well and played a mean rhythm guitar. Like Peter, Chrissie was a songwriter who used unusual song structures and who put together a fine rock 'n' roll band to play her songs. Unlike The Only Ones, the Pretenders were successful from their first single, the Ray Davies' obscurity 'Stop Your Sobbing'. Two commercially and artistically successful LPs followed, *Pretenders* (1980) and *Pretenders II* (1981).

So why did the Pretenders make it while The Only Ones didn't? It certainly wasn't drug-related: Honeyman-Scott OD'd and bass player Pete Farndon was sacked for dope-related unreliability. Dave Hill's experienced management, a sympathetic record company and an ambitious and hard-working front person had more to do with it. Ironically, in March 1982 The Pretenders asked Alan Mair to take over from Farndon. Alan still regrets that he was unable to take the job: it would have been an admission that The Only Ones had broken up, defaulting on their contract with CBS in the process and leaving them to repay their considerable recording advance. The band had to wait for CBS to drop them, which they did.

If Peter had been less antagonistic towards CBS, if the band had signed to Island, if 'Planet' had been played more on the radio …who knows? What is certain is that *The Only Ones* still burns bright today and if you are coming to it fresh I envy you being able to hear these wonderful performances for the very first time.

'I think I'm on another world with you, with you …'

BIBLIOGRAPHY

All interviews conducted with the author unless otherwise specified.

Antonia, Nina (1996) *The One and Only: Peter Perrett, Homme Fatale*, SAF Publishing

Antonia, Nina (2005) England's Glory – The First and Last sleeve notes

Antonia, Nina (2020) interview

Batsford, Stuart (2020) interview

Bell, Max (1978) 'Peter Perrett Picked a Peck of Pickled Peppers', *NME*

Brickle, Steve (2005) MySpace

Buskin, Richard (2007) 'Classic Tracks: Another Girl Another Planet' *Sound On Sound*

Dadomo, Giovanni (1978) 'Another Year, Another Planet' *Sounds*

Garner, Ken (1993) *In Session Tonight: The Complete Radio 1 Recordings*, BBC Books

Gravelle, Peter (2020) interview

Heylin, Clinton (2016) *Anarchy In The Year Zero*, Route

Impey, Lawrence (2020) interview

Kellie, Mike (2013) *Village Times – Brewood, Coven and Bishops Wood* quoted on www.mikekellie.com

Kellie, Mike (2016) interview

Lawson, Martin (2001) Peter Perrett Discography 1973 – 2000

Lillywhite, Steve (2018) interviewed by Tim Somer for www.rockandroll.globe.com,

Mair, Alan (2020) interview
Makowski, Pete (2020) interview
Newey, Jon (2005) England's Glory – The First and Last sleevenotes
Newey, Jon (2020) interview
Perrett, Peter (1977) *Sounds*
Perrett, Peter (2015) interviewed by Thomas H. Green for *The Arts Desk*
Perrett, Peter (2017) interviewed by Peter Jesperson for www.kexp.org
Perrett, Peter (2020) interviewed by Amy Haben for www.pleasekillme.com
Perrett, Peter (2021) interview
Perry, John (2006-7) MySpace
Perry, John (2020) interview
Pinnock, Tom (2015) *Uncut*
Tygier, John (2020) interview
Whitfield, Bob (2020) interview
Williams, Paul (1993) *Rock and Roll: The 100 Best Singles*, Entwhistle Books
Wright, Simon (2007) 'Band, Interrupted – the return of The Only Ones', *Bucketfull of Brains*

Lightning Source UK Ltd.
Milton Keynes UK
UKHW051610230223
417464UK00010BA/103